"future" books; he believes that there *are* choices.

Mr. Lundborg never loses his perspective or his sense of humor. His book will ruffle many feathers, but it offers comfort to those who are willing to face facts.

Louis B. Lundborg continues as director of the Bank of America and several other major companies. He runs a TV show on business and its problems; he is chairman of the board of trustees of the Huntington Library and a director of Stanford Research Institute.

Born in Billings, Montana, Mr. Lundborg was a research chemist, a bookkeeper, worked in chambers of commerce, and served as vice president in charge of university development at Stanford University, before joining the Bank of America.

Mr. Lundborg lives with his wife in Ross, California.

FUTURE
WITHOUT
SHOCK

FUTURE
WITHOUT
SHOCK

LOUIS B. LUNDBORG

W·W·NORTON&COMPANY·INC·

NEW YORK

Copyright © 1974 by W. W. Norton & Company, Inc.

All Rights Reserved

Published simultaneously in Canada
by George J. McLeod Limited, Toronto

Library of Congress Cataloging in Publication Data

Lundborg, Louis B
Future without shock.

1. United States—Social conditions—1960–
2. Social change. 3. Social values. I. Title.
HN59.L85   309.1′73′092   73–14645
ISBN 0–393–05504–3

"Time," page 45, Lyric through the courtesy of Aurelius Music from "Does
Anybody Know What Time It Is?" by Robert Lamm.
"Live for Today," page 45. Copyright © 1966 Edizoni Musicali, RCA
Italiana, Rome. Used by permission. All Rights Reserved.

Printed in the United States of America

3 4 5 6 7 8 9 0

To the two BWL's—
one because he insisted I start this and
the other because she insisted I finish it.

CONTENTS

ACKNOWLEDGMENTS

When a book has grown, as this one has, out of a wide range of experiences and over a long span of years, it is impossible to identify all those who have played a part in its development. The list would have to include all the teachers, relatives, counselors, co-workers, and friends who have made some contribution to my knowledge or understanding.

So I must limit myself to acknowledging my debt to those who have been most immediately helpful to me in the period of my writing of the book.

To James F. Langton I am doubly indebted: not only have his suggestions on the structure and the content of the book been wise and helpful, but over a span of years his perceptive reactions to events and ideas have helped to sharpen my own sensitivity to the issues covered here.

Bernard L. Butcher has saved me countless hours in research and assembling of materials; and so has William T. Hull by sharing the results of research he had done for his graduate thesis.

And if it has not been for James S. Young, I might never have been introduced to the world of student thought and opinion.

FUTURE
WITHOUT
SHOCK

THE GREENING OF
A BANKER

1

Yogi Berra, the longtime catcher and dugout philosopher of New York major-league baseball teams, was once quoted as saying, "You can observe a lot just by watching."

He might have added, "You can hear a lot just by listening."

From where I sat for many years as a senior officer and finally as chairman of the board of the world's largest bank, I had a unique opportunity to "observe a lot and hear a lot" about what was happening in our society. Furthermore, the circumstances were such that even if I had wanted to I could not have enjoyed the luxury of just watching and listening—just sitting up in the bleachers as a spectator. For the years of my chairmanship of Bank of America happened to coincide with the years of the greatest turbulence and social upheaval that our country has seen in a century. Our bank became involved in one after another of the major expressions of this turbulence; and then I became personally involved in ways that compelled me to do more than just watch and listen. I was obliged to think, too.

These were the years when the racial tensions in our black ghettos—and later our brown barrios—boiled up into the "hot summers" of Watts, Detroit, Newark, and other large cities; the years of campus unrest and riots; the years when youth in general was jolting the elders with its revolt against the established mores; when corporations were being challenged, as never before, to prove that they were operating in the best interest of society; when the words "environment" and "ecology" were taking on new meaning as symbols of a growing concern that quality of life was being sacrificed to so-called progress; and when the bitterly unpopular war in Vietnam was driving deep wedges of discord into every level of our society.

On each of these and many lesser issues I found myself having to take a public position, either as spokesman for the bank in a direct confrontation or in concert with other business, civic, and political leaders when the turmoil was on a broader front—or even when there were no such constraints on me, but when my own convictions impelled me to speak out personally, as I did in April of 1970 when I testified before the Senate Foreign Relations Committee in opposition to our involvement in Vietnam.

Thinking about each of these issues and trying to understand them led me to dig a little deeper than I ever had done before into what lay behind them, and to reflect on what might lie ahead. I learned that anyone who embarks with an open mind on such a journey of inquiry and reflection must be prepared for surprises. My conclusions were not at all what I had expected at the outset.

I also learned that anyone who sets out on such a journey should not stop midway. The first discoveries are the most jolting and disturbing, but when they are pursued further even the most unsettling developments are seen not to be all bad—in fact, they are seen to hold the brightest hope for our future.

It became plain to me that the new value system surfacing in America has so changed our country that it will never be the same again. And further changes will jar and shake most of the assumptions we all have grown up with: new

concepts of private property, new attitudes toward growth
and "progress," and new standards of social responsibility.

Some people, and some companies, will not learn to cope
with these changes. They will fall by the wayside.

But those who do learn to cope—or better still, those
who learn to understand the real meaning of these changes
so that they become part of the best of the new pattern—
will find it a time of highly rewarding and satisfying potential. If enough people and their companies make the
adjustment—and I think they ultimately will—it can be
one of the most richly rewarding eras in the history of our
society. But it will be quite a different era from the one we
envisioned as we entered the Fabulous Fifties and the
Soaring Sixties.

As we have done several times before in our national
history, we have come again to a major crossroads, a historically crucial turning point in the course of our society.
We have heard dire warnings of all the disasters that lie
ahead of us. I am sure that all those dread consequences are
possible; but I am not convinced that they are inevitable.
I believe that there *are* choices.

To help to identify those choices is the purpose of this
book.

Because the young were early and vocal advocates of
change, and because my own awareness of the dimensions
of that change grew out of my confrontations with young
people, I have devoted the early chapters of the book to the
observations and reflections that developed out of those
confrontations.

But because the vast sweep of social change taking place
around us is by no means limited to the young—the process
includes our whole society—I have endeavored to interpret
what these movements mean to *all* the people of this
country.

Certain fields that have been conspicuous arenas of public debate I have singled out for special emphasis, as in the

chapters on the corporation and on the environment—not just because they have special importance, which they do, but because I was close enough to them to see that they are microcosms of the broader concerns of our entire society.

This book does not profess to provide answers to all the problems of society. If I had the wisdom and the temerity to address such an awesome undertaking, the product could not be compressed into a dozen volumes the size of this one.

It is my hope, however, and my earnest belief that some of the principles I have endeavored to distill out of my experience can apply with equal force to problems and issues that I have not mentioned at all in this volume. Principles and policies are constructed out of attitudes; the attitudes that I trust will be apparent to the reader of this book I would commend as approaches to the exciting days we have ahead of us.

Finally, if this book "comforts the disturbed and disturbs the comfortable" it will have served a large part of its purpose.

THE LESSONS OF
ISLA VISTA

2

When the waters tumble over the face of Niagara Falls and crash with a deafening roar on the rocks below, those waters don't originate at Niagara and they don't end there. They have their sources in lakes and brooks and mountain streams hundreds of miles away, and they flow on down through Lake Ontario and the St. Lawrence River and finally into the Atlantic Ocean. Their by-product—the power generated at the Falls—finds its way into factories, offices, and homes all across the eastern part of the United States and Canada.

So it was with the campus unrest and violence that exploded all over America in the late 1960s and reached their peak with the killing of four students at Kent State University in Ohio in May of 1970. Only small fragments of that uprising had their beginnings anywhere near the campus where they exploded; the shock waves vibrated out from there across all of America and most of the world.

The many commissions and committees created to inquire into the causes of that wave of unrest have filled countless thick volumes with their reports. Little purpose would be served now in rehashing what was in those reports except as backdrop for what has happened since, what is going on around us now, and what seems to be in the offing.

While in each local situation there were special issues and grievances—of a kind that in an earlier day would have been the subject of an editorial in the campus daily, or at the most the occasion for heated discussion in the councils of the student government, followed possibly by a committee calling upon the president or the dean—there were a few universal themes that ran through all the outbursts.

Clearly the dominant issue everywhere, and the one that provided enough emotional fuel to build up fever-heat in one area after another, was Vietnam. A war that was not very popular in any age group hit with special impact on the young. They were being called upon to disrupt their lives—and lay down their lives—in a cause that they did not believe in, that they thought was manifestly immoral in itself and doubly so when their involvement in it was being forced upon them. Their feelings of outrage, compounded by feelings of impotence and frustration because they could see no way to get out of their entrapment in it, led in many instances to an angry impulse to strike back at whoever was imposing this hideous thing on them—someone called "the Establishment."

Naturally, anything else the Establishment was doing wrong—the Establishment by this time being an umbrella term that covered the Government, the Administration of the college, the Faculty, Business, and the Older Generation in general—was added to the indictment whenever inflammatory speeches were made at rallies.

What none of us seemed to realize at the time—and this was never to my knowledge brought out in the ample press coverage of the turbulent period—was that this was not a new experience for America. In fact, as Lowell H. Harrison revealed in an article in *American History Illustrated* entitled "Rowdies, Riots and Rebellions," from the period of the American Revolution right up to the Civil War—during the first eighty-five years of our national existence—student unrest was "more prevalent and more violent than in any other period of our history prior to the 1960s."

Most dramatic of the incidents that Harrison recounts was the "Riotous Commencement" at Columbia in 1811, when a senior student delivered an inflammatory address, and was refused his diploma. His classmates pushed him back on the platform, the provost called the city marshal, but students overwhelmed the police, the faculty was put into flight, and students held possession of the church where the commencement took place.

President Wheelock of Dartmouth commented on this incident: "Melancholy must be the prospect of the future state of our country when those of the rising generation . . . undertake to insult humanity and justice, to prostrate the laws and overturn the social order."

In 1851, the University of North Carolina had an enrollment of 230; during the year the faculty dealt with 282 cases of delinquent behavior.

In 1841, Yale students defeated New Haven firemen in a brawl, destroying their equipment. In 1807, at Princeton, half the student body was suspended.

Twenty years later the University of Virginia was the scene of student riots, with armed and masked students patrolling the campus. College presidents were shot, stabbed, and bombed; a Yale professor armed himself with two pistols for an entire summer.

Student unrest is as old as the earliest medieval universities. What is new are the reasons and rationalizations on the one hand, and the aftermath on the other.

Always before, the incidents had been localized and had seemed to grow out of purely local issues. While Harrison does not say so, it is probable that the earlier episodes were largely a rebellion of youth against parental authority, an activity that has gone on everywhere since the beginning of time and is a necessary part of the growing-up process.

By 1800, we are told, "students were becoming more insistent upon being treated as 'gentlemen' and upon receiving their 'rights.' . . . This new radicalism clashed directly with the traditional concept of students' status and the rigid disciplinary codes which college officials had formulated to control their charges."

It is probably just as well that most of the current adult generation has forgotten that earlier history, for if we had known it, we might have been inclined to pass this newest wave off as just another instance of youthful rebellion against parental authority. That would have been a grave mistake.

The classic kind of youth rebellion was, of course, an element in all the disturbances, and that at least made the emotional climate right for everything that followed. But I was convinced at the time—and it now has become quite clear—that what was happening went far, far beyond that.

My own involvement with this question began very abruptly in early 1970 when a rampaging mob of demonstrators—some students, some non-students—set fire to the Bank of America branch at Isla Vista adjoining the University of California, Santa Barbara campus, and totally destroyed it. The demonstration originally was not aimed at the bank at all, but was an angry attack on "the capitalist establishment." Since the bank was the most conspicuous example of the "establishment"—almost the only one in this small college community—it became a convenient target.

My first reaction, and that of my bank colleagues, was one of understandable anger and, to be trite, "righteous indignation." We expressed that indignation in television and radio appearances, press conferences, and full-page newspaper ads, which I signed, carried throughout California and later all across the country. Factually (with minor exceptions due to the haste of our first pronouncements) we were absolutely correct, but in retrospect I was compelled to acknowledge that the angry tone was counter-productive. When friends asked me, months later, what I would do if I had it to do over—would I say the same thing? —my reply was that I might say most of the same things, but not in such an angry tone. Which means that they *wouldn't*, in fact, have been the same things.

Our friends, and any others who were already outraged by the mob attack, applauded our pronouncements; I doubt that they changed many minds. They may even have driven some groups into animosity toward us who might other-wise have remained more sympathetic toward us.

The one most valid criticism of our total posture came from some of our business friends who remarked, "Oh, yeah. You are very indignant when *you* are damaged. There has been violence before. Where were you then?" To which we could only reply, "*Touché.*"

In the weeks that followed, I found myself plunged into a succession of confrontations, meetings, and conversations with student groups in an effort to gain some understanding of what was happening. Interspersed between the meetings with students were several sessions with presidents, faculty, and administrators of California colleges and universities.

It would have surprised the students to know that what I heard from the officers and faculty members was not as different from the average views of the students (if one can speak of "averaging" such views) as the extremes of the student views differed from each other.

The very diversity that characterized the student group was also what made them much more fun to tangle with—even if at times I was not sure I could hold my own with them.

The most memorable—and most exhausting—of all these encounters was one that fell into my lap through a piece of good fortune. A young student-body president of one of the state colleges called me one day to tell me that his executive committee wanted to close out its student-body account with the Bank of America; he felt that they had swallowed whole a lot of anti-Establishment half-truths that had been circulated and parroted around ever since the Isla Vista burning; he disagreed with many of the things they were saying and had tried to defend Bank of America, particularly against the boycott idea, but he had run out of ammunition and wondered if I could help him.

After talking with him for more than a half hour by telephone, I said, "Jim, instead of my trying to answer all your questions by telephone, why don't you come in to town and have lunch with me, where we can go into more of the background of all this?"

He agreed, we made a date, and he came. But I was hardly prepared for what greeted me. It is amusing to me now to look back and see how three years have changed our outlook on so many things that seemed grimly important then. People were still being apoplectic over long hair and beards then. So when a young man with hair down to his shoulders—the first of his kind I had ever met face to face —appeared at my office to accept my invitation to luncheon at the Stock Exchange Club, I gulped! But Stock Exchange Club I had said, so to Stock Exchange Club we went. For days afterward, friends would greet me on the street with gibes that each one thought was original, all variations on the theme: "Louis, was that your son I saw you eating lunch with—or your daughter?"

But I would not trade that day for anything I did in that whole year. For out of that luncheon visit grew not only a warm friendship with a fine young man, but an introduction—an entrée—into the new world of the youth culture that, a few weeks before, I had scarcely known existed. I have not "bought" everything I have seen of that culture, but neither have I rejected it all; and I could not have been intelligent in evaluating, discussing, encouraging, or discouraging any of it if I did not even know what it was.

Soon after our luncheon, Jim called me one day to ask

if I would be interested in meeting with some of the other student-body presidents from other state colleges. I jumped at the chance, and Jim proceeded to try to get them together. I never did learn exactly how he communicated with them, or exactly how they got to Los Angeles from colleges as much as five hundred miles away. I had already learned that communication between campuses all across this country would put to shame any other known grapevine. The unofficial grapevine centered around office watercoolers is more efficient than official channels, but this one beats that.

One young man has boasted to one of my associates that he can get a message to New York faster than we could get it there by air mail, and without using any normal means of communications, simply by using their grapevine. But I also had learned not to ask too many questions about how it was done.

However it was done, the young presidents arrived from the major institutions all up and down the state. And this was the encounter that turned out to be so much fun and so exhausting—both for the same reason. These were among the liveliest minds I met in all my contacts with young people. In one sense they were a microcosm of all students, and in another sense they were a very special sample. They were obviously more extroverted than the average—or they wouldn't have been involved and successful in student politics—but they were probably a fair sample of the political and ideological coloration of all their constituencies. They ranged from the young Mexican-American (we were just learning the term "Chicano" then) who was an openly avowed revolutionary ("I'm out to destroy your system") to the lad from an agriculturally oriented college who said, "My parents were immigrants who came to America with nothing but have been able to give me a good education. America has been very good to my family and to me. I don't see what all the ranting is about." In between was every shade of the spectrum, but if we had constructed the bell curve, so popular in their college courses, the bulge would have been around those who didn't want to destroy the system but wanted to change it pretty drastically; who didn't want to do anything violently but wanted affirmative and positive action—and action right now.

The one thing the members of this group shared in common was a willingness—and an ability—to talk. I could see reflected in our dialogue the hours they must have spent in what my generation called bull sessions and this generation called rap sessions. Socrates and Plato had done it with their friends, Samuel Johnson had done it with his, and these young people had done it—without creating any deathless pearls of dialectic brilliance, to be sure, but with enough readiness and persuasiveness to get themselves elected.

And all this skill they turned loose on me, putting me through an inquisition about everything the corporate world was doing wrong or failing to do right. A few of these charges I had heard before, but many were new. Most of them I was to hear over and over in the weeks to come, because, in the fashion of all ideological rhetoric, certain allegations and even certain stock phrases would get picked up and repeated over and over: why did the bank lend money to the government of South Africa; why did it lend money to war contractors; why did it, and other corporations, not hire more blacks? (Because our bank had a good record on its total hiring of minorities, including blacks, and was working hard to build training programs that would bring more of these people up into executive ranks, I got fairly good marks on this one, but was told, "You still haven't done enough"—a statement with which I, and my colleagues back at the office, could all agree.) It is interesting to me now to look back and realize that Women's Lib had not made visible inroads on that group; no concern was expressed then, as it often was later, for the unequal treatment of women.

By a wide margin the most attractive person in that group was the young Chicano revolutionary. Handsome by any standard, brimming with vitality, he was the kind of male animal who would be equally attractive to men or women. Anyone who had grown up with the old cartoon stereotype of the revolutionist in his mind—the grim Bolshevik with thick-lensed glasses—would be doubly startled by this lad, because he capped all his other attributes with a breezy (what my generation would call "cocky") good humor. He would grin at me and say, "You're a nice guy— but you're part of a dead system. Your days are numbered."

I thought then, and have thought many times since, that if there ever is a revolution in this country, my young friend Raul will be right up there with the leaders, and he'll be followed at least by everyone who comes under the influence of his infectious personality.

But neither that day nor in any of my later encounters did I find any reason to think that revolution, of the kind he envisioned, is what faces this country. What we face may be—I think it will be—"revolutionary" in the sense of sweeping change coming so fast that it upsets and overturns many long-established patterns of behavior and relationships. I think it will be, in fact, because it already has started and will continue. Our world will never be the same again. But as revolutionary as the changes will be, the methods by which they are brought about need not be violent; at least the campus riots of the 1960s and early 1970s, I am convinced, offer no reason to expect mass violence.

Both of these convictions—of the extent of the change, and of the methods by which it will be brought about— grow out of everything that has happened to me since the burning at Isla Vista: the conclusions that I drew out of my many encounters and confrontations in the early months after the burning; then the findings of the several official commissions and committees, which tended to confirm my own observations; and finally my continuing contact with the academic community at several levels and at several locations.

Meanwhile the incidents of violence and destruction went on—most of them hit-and-run actions like the tossing of fire bombs into buildings, but some of major proportions. In our own bank alone the incidents were averaging more than one a day somewhere in our statewide system (once we had been adopted as the symbol of the hateful Establishment, we became a convenient target throughout California.) Many of these were relatively minor—a rock through a plate glass window, a Molotov cocktail through a front door, a fire started in a lobby wastebasket and ruining the interior paint with smoke—but the climax was an incident far more tragic than mere property damage.

After our Isla Vista branch was burned, we decided we would reopen in temporary quarters. This was a debatable decision and indeed it was hotly debated, both inside the bank and out. Many of the law-enforcement and university administration officials advised against reopening, on the ground that it would be a challenge, an incitement to more violence. We were aware of this hazard, but the converse hazard was that if we failed to reopen, we would encourage the notion that lawless mobs anywhere could dictate who could operate and where and under what terms. We were, after all, a public service institution, chartered by the federal government to serve the community, and while that was a privilege we had sought, it also was an obligation.

So the conclusion was to reopen in temporary quarters and to announce at the same time that we would start immediately to build new and enlarged permanent quarters on the site of the ones that had been burned.

As predicted, the opening of the temporary branch in mobile units triggered a new wave of incidents, small at first, but building up to the night when a street rally turned into another mob demand to march on the bank and burn it down again. This time, when they marched and closed in on the bank, there were students opposing them and defending the bank, along with a force of sheriff's deputies. In the resulting fracas, while fires were being started by one group and being stamped out by others, and while the two groups were battling each other, a shot was fired. One of the students, Kevin Moran, who had been trying to put out the fires, was shot and killed.

It never has been determined with any certainty who fired the shot. There were charges that a sniper had shot from a building across the street, and other charges that a sheriff's deputy had done it. One of the deputies acknowledged that his gun had been discharged—accidentally, according to his report—but denied any knowledge of it hitting anyone. The one certainty was that if there had been no riot, there would have been no shooting.

While that tragedy seemed to have some sobering effect on the trend toward mob action, the hostility was still smoldering many weeks thereafter. So it was in that setting that I was called upon one day to answer the question: Were there any lessons that could be drawn from the period of turbulence, of violence and destruction, that we had been passing through?

As I recite them now, I have to remind myself that we were still in a state of explosive tension. Tempers were hot on all sides: among student and youth leaders, among those in the community who were dealing with them, plus all the kibitzers on the sidelines who were sure they knew just how the problem should be handled. The remedies proposed by this latter group smacked strongly of vigilantism, and were one of the most dangerous elements in the entire situation.

Sorting out all the angry cross-currents that still were swirling around, I concluded that the lessons were several, they were subtle, they were complex. If they were viewed literally as lessons, they were like many other lessons of life—easier to say in words than to follow in practice. But also like many other lessons of life, they would be ignored at our peril. What were they? I listed them as follows:

1. While destruction may have been committed by a violent few, and may have been led by even fewer, the underlying feelings that gave rise to the violence are much more pervasive.

2. Although unrest over Vietnam is the most obvious cause of the activism, there are many other issues that will not go away even after Vietnam. We are facing a real, honest-to-God disenchantment—not just a passing, momentary flare-up, that will go away if we can just keep it cool for a while.

3. We still have to cool it—and that won't be easy.

4. The violence must be rejected but the dissent and protest must not be.

5. There is a new value system emerging in America, starting with the youth but becoming one of the new facts of life for the rest of us to deal with.

6. Our dealing with it will jar us out of most of the comfortable assumptions that we have grown up with all of our lives.

Let's look at these one at a time and then see what they add up to for each of us.

Perhaps one of the greatest errors many of us have been guilty of has been the tendency to assume that all the airing of grievances, all the resultant disturbances, can be laid at the door of an extremely small, fanatically militant hardcore minority. That such an assumption is comfortable in no way changes the fact that it is also grossly inaccurate.

While the actual burning of our Isla Vista branch may have been perpetrated by a violent few, there is no question that there was widespread agreement among the students on the Santa Barbara campus that the causes leading to the protest were both serious and legitimate. Apparently a substantial majority of the campus community deplored the use of violent action. But an almost equally substantial majority sympathized with and shared in the frustrations leading to that violence.

This phenomenon has been observed elsewhere. Following the student takeover of Cornell's Willard Straight Hall in April 1969, the university retained an opinion-research firm to study underlying campus attitudes about the incident. The findings are both illuminating and disturbing.

In response to a question concerning how widespread campus dissatisfaction was, there was substantial agreement that the incident reflected a "ground swell" of unrest among the majority of students.

The basic attitudes and leanings underlying these incidents were reflected in a recent Gallup Poll in which students and adults across the country were asked to classify themselves as "liberal" or "conservative." The students overwhelmingly—by a ratio of more than 2 to 1—labeled themselves liberal, while the adults—by a ratio of 3 to 2—identified themselves as conservative.

Any doubt that was left on this score disappeared after the tragedy at Kent State and the entry into Cambodia, when the dissension became virtually unanimous on campus after campus all over America.

In the months that followed, reports appeared from the several commissions and committees that had been searching into the causes of this wave of unrest. While each one approached the problem from a slightly different angle, and so put differing emphasis on the several contributing causes, they all were in essential agreement with each other and tended to confirm my own conclusions. One would give more weight to social tensions and the problems of the minorities, while another would lay more stress on the "personal-freedom" urge of youth. But they all acknowledged the prime role of Vietnam in supplying the emotional fuel.

Whether any such activism would eventually have developed in America even if there had been no Vietnam, we shall never know. But it is quite clear to me that it was our involvement in Vietnam that triggered it, and that each passing year and each additional degree of entanglement increased the bitterness and intensity of the feeling. Students who might otherwise have been quite passive about other issues became inflamed over this one.

Feeling trapped by their elders into an immoral war, and feeling impotent and frustrated in all their attempts to make themselves heard, these young people began to question everything their elders were doing, and to question everything about the society another generation had created.

It was a little like the Internal Revenue man who finds a flaw in an income tax return, and then begins to dig in and question everything about the whole return.

Whatever caused Pandora's Box to be opened—whether the eternal rebellion of youth or the special problem of Vietnam—the issues that have come spilling out of Pandora's Box are not going to be stuffed back in.

This is the part of the lessons of Isla Vista that remains most alive in the perspective of three years.

The necessity to "cool it" and the imperative necessity to reject violence were early recognized by the great majority of the students.

Even before Vietnam began to wind down, the violence had cooled, but that didn't mean that the danger of new outbreaks had disappeared. The danger remained just below the surface, as we learned after the bombing of Hanoi and Haiphong was renewed. I shall tell more in a later chapter about the incidents that occurred then; let me simply say now that these later incidents were not supported by the majority of students, who by now had condemned violence as an instrument of campus policy.

Other dangers that had been very real at the time when campus unrest and violence were at their height had also largely dissipated. I remarked after our branch was burned that I was not afraid that the left-wing radicals would win in their revolutionary efforts; I was only afraid of how they would be defeated. The natural sequel to left-wing rebellion is right-wing reaction and repression. History shows only too plainly that repression doesn't repress only the bad guys; it ends by controlling and repressing everyone—particularly everyone who disagrees with the party in power.

There were many people who were saying, during the peak of the riots, "Maybe we should let some blood flow. We are never going to settle this thing until we have it out and show who's really running things around here." That could have been the end of America as we have known it. It could have been the end of the American dream.

Fortunately, it never happened. In spite of all the blunders that may have been made by peace officers trying to handle situations for which many of them were ill-prepared, and in spite of any police brutality or other excesses of which any of them may have been guilty, with significant but special exceptions the effort at peace-keeping and control was not allowed to slip out of the hands of the regularly constituted forces acting under the authority of law.

That is an achievement that should not be discounted—either in difficulty or in importance.

Maintaining the cool throughout the nation was made no easier by the inflammatory remarks that issued from certain high places in our government. It was a time of tension, and what we needed was a soft voice—a collective soft voice. In the 1968 election we had been promised that, and we were promised a national effort to bring us closer again. Instead, we heard too many angry words, too much name-calling.

Thanks to the many superb people in key spots who did have the necessary qualities, and who helped to cool the country down, the "generation gap" polarization that was beginning to take shape at the time of the worst riots did not proceed far and does not today appear to be *the* significant issue. This is not to say that new polarizing has not begun on other issues.

One reason we are not so divided is that the lines separating us have become blurred and dim with the passage of time. Issues that seemed crucial in 1968 became so faded that it is hard to believe they were ever important. In fact, it is tragicomic to look back and realize that it was not the really big issues that got the blood pressure of the elders up to near-apoplexy level. I swear that there was more emotional heat generated over length of hair and manner of dress than there was over the most extreme violence. The burnings, the bombings, and the vandalism left many older Americans bewildered, but these same people knew exactly how to react to the long hair, the beards, the guitars, and the beads. Those trappings were a direct affront to oldsters because they meant that the youth were daring to be different and were flaunting their differentness.

Even at the time, I was more amused than disturbed by the preoccupation with hair and beards. I remarked once that when I sat in my customary seat in the boardroom of the Los Angeles Clearing House, I saw on the wall facing me portraits of all the presidents of the Clearing House. Of course, the early half of them all had beards.

And I chuckle when I recall that during that same period we seriously debated whether we should have a dress code in the bank that would specify how long hair could be, and how short the skirts, and whether pants suits would be permitted on women. It was lucky for us that we decided such a code wouldn't work—because it wouldn't have. At best, we would have been laughed at by our employees; at worst we might have had a strike.

Today, long hair is such an accepted fact that it is no longer an issue at all. In the executive suite we refer to it as "hair styling" and it costs about five times as much as a regular haircut, but whatever it is called and whatever it costs, it is one case in which the young have taught us that it is possible to "do your own thing" in matters that do no harm to others.

(I confess that I think slightly longer hair is becoming to most men, so much so that the "white side walls" of the past fifty years actually look a little insipid. But again, that is only a matter of personal taste, and I have no right to impose it on anyone else!)

AWAY FROM THE VOLCANO

3

It is foolish to generalize about youth, to say that "the young" are any one thing. They are everything—except old. They are radical, they are conservative; they are industrious and lazy; serious and funloving; business-oriented and arts-oriented; militarist and pacifist—and so on through the catalog.

Young people, like all other people, range across the complete scale of political, philosophical, and cultural attitudes. They differ from older groups in that theirs is a learning period, a time of growth, so that their views might change from month to month and from year to year. At any one point in time, if we were to chart the attitudes of a thousand college students on any popular issue, we might find them clustering more thickly around one position than would a thousand older people; and that position might be considerably to left or right of the cluster-point of the older group.

More important than their position at a single point in time, though, is the direction in which they are moving. This we find well documented in surveys such as the one Daniel Yankelovich, Inc., did in 1972 for the JDR Third Fund titled "The Changing Values on Campus." In its profile of political and personal attitudes of today's college students, it reveals many surprising, even startling, findings, and it highlights other points which, while not as surprising, are far-reaching in their significance.

Those who have thought that the protest and dissent of the late 1960s were just a momentary flurry that would soon blow over will get little comfort from this study. It is true that there is less support for *political* radicalism than there was in the earlier period, but the changes in cultural values —attitudes toward marriage, authority, religion, work, money, career, sexual mores, and other aspects of the Puritan Ethic—have become more marked and more dramatic.

This separation of cultural values from political values has not taken place among students who identify themselves with the New Left. For these students, the life-styles of the Counter Culture and radical politics go together. "But the vast majority of students—the 89 percent who do not identify with the New Left—have pressed forward in their search for a cultural revolution while taking a step backwards from political revolution," the Yankelovich survey continues.

The current crop of students are described as no less serious than their predecessors, no less disenchanted with traditional values, and no less determined to reshape society.

The survey describes the current student mood as "confused but not despairing," but points out that the shift in mood away from the despair and depression reported a year earlier does not mean that students feel any better about the state of our society. On the contrary, they are more uneasy and worried than before. More of them than in previous years think we have a sick society on our hands.

The business and economic views of the students are a strange mixture of Marxian and free-enterprise–capitalist values. A majority believe that the real power in the country is vested in big business and the great financial institutions, and accept the Marxian view that our system of government is democratic in name only—that the mass of people are propagandized into believing that what the public thinks really counts.

But side by side with these views is the belief expressed by a whopping 85 percent of all students that business is entitled to make a profit. Seventy percent subscribe to the traditional belief that the holding of private property is valid.

Overall, there is less rather than more polarization among students than in recent years. Students seem less dogmatic in their beliefs on both ends of the political spectrum, they are becoming more pragmatic—and pragmatism has been the genius of America.

As an example of the current diversity of opinion, studies show that the majority of students are disenchanted with economic imperatives, with "growth for growth's sake"; but that blacks and other minority groups, who still seek after economic enrichment, do not share this disenchantment.

During and after the period of greatest militancy and unrest, the majority of students felt—and continue to feel —that the United States is too materialistic and conformist, and many believe that *all* our troubles stem from making economic competition the basis of our way of life.

One of the continuing sources of frustration and anger among the young is that, in spite of this apparent concentration on economic imperatives, they are faced with a lack of job opportunities.

Usually when we oldsters talk about our youth and compare our experiences with those of today's generation, we like to tell about how much harder things were then—to prove, of course, how much tougher and hardier we are than today's soft young. But as one who worked his entire way through college (and never felt martyred about it, because most of my contemporaries did some degree of the same) I have to testify that it was a lot easier then. Jobs were relatively more plentiful, and they were closer at hand.

The communities surrounding our colleges were not to-day's metropolises; we didn't have to travel fifty miles—or more—a day between home, school and job; and the potential employers were not so largely local branches of large chain organizations.

On another front, a substantial increase is reported in the number of students who believe that marriage is obsolete, and who accept the propriety of premarital sexual relations, extramarital sexual relations, and homosexuality between consenting adults. (The survey does not express a judgment on this trend or attempt to trace its origins. Another study, however, to which I shall refer in the next chapter, describes modern youth as ignorant of history. While this comment was made in a different context, it could well apply equally here: in rebelling against institutionally imposed disciplines, youth seems to ignore that not all the restraints came out of Puritan influence nor were as arbitrarily inspired as many Puritan doctrines were. Particularly those relating to marriage have their roots deep in the history of civilized cultures; whatever variations and modifications may have been adopted from time to time have not for long displaced the family as a stabilizing social force.)

On other morality issues there are some surprising contrasts. More students think it is immoral to collect welfare when one is capable of working than believe it morally wrong to work one's way through college by selling dope. Pilferage—taking things without paying for them—ranks high among immoral actions.

While a massive revulsion is reported by Yankelovich against the idea of violence, there is, today, surprising student acceptance of tactics verging on overt violence, such as blockades, ultimatums, and sit-ins.

One hardly needs a survey of opinion to know that the potential for violence is still only an inch below the surface. Even though the wave of destructive violence of the late sixties and early seventies was committed by a tiny percentage of students (plus a coterie of non-student "street people"); even though the great majority of students then expressed abhorrence for violence as an instrument of protest, a view that is even more pronounced today; and even though the campus mood remained quiet for nearly two years after "peaking out" in the Kent State tragedy, it is only too apparent how fragile such quiet can be: when President Nixon ordered the bombing of Hanoi and Haiphong after the 1972 elections, it was the signal for a "spontaneous combustion" all over the country. Berkeley, which had been the scene of the earliest and among the most frequent of student uprisings, suffered the worst "trashing" of its history: broken windows, paint-smeared store fronts, uprooted landscaping, overturned and mutilated automobiles all through its business district and beyond. The trashers were relatively few in number, compared with the huge mobs of the earlier riots, but they were numerous enough, and violent enough, to do an ugly job of vandalizing.

Like most of the destruction in this entire era of the sixties and seventies, it was mindless, because the damage was inflicted on those who could not have been considered even remotely responsible for the actions that were being protested.

But unlike the earlier depredations, this one did not seem to attract even the "audience support" of the morbidly curious onlookers. One of the contributing factors to the effectiveness of the earlier mobs was the degree to which crowds of bystanders, originally drawn by curiosity, were themselves drawn into the action and fanned into mob frenzy by the leaders. This time they stayed away, and the damage was done by the hardcore radicals, including the non-student "street people."

As evidence of how mindless much of this vandalism was, I cite a case that involved our bank. Nearly a year after the burning of our branch at Isla Vista, we were still having incidents throughout California at the rate of two or three a week of the kind we had come to consider "minor" because they involved only a few thousand dollars each in damage. But there were no confrontations and no announced grievances, just the hit-and-run variety of depredation. After two neighboring branches in suburban Marin County had been damaged within a few hours of each other by the explosion of crudely made bombs, a sixteen-year-old high school boy was arrested on a tip-off to the police and promptly confessed. When asked why he had done it, his only rationale was, "Well, gee whiz . . . all the other guys were doing it!"

Even this adolescent kind of interest in playing "follow-the-leader" was largely dissipated by the time of the 1972 Berkeley trashing.

When I inquired into the reasons for this change of mood, I found no better explanation than one given me by a young businessman, five years out of college, whose professional job is interviewing and recruiting graduating students for a large corporation. He said, "At the time of the Kevin Moran and the Kent State shootings, students had crawled to the edge of the volcano and were looking straight down into the fire. They didn't like what they saw. They were sickened by the thought of what they had already helped to perpetrate, and horrified to think how close they had come to something infinitely worse. They just backed away from that volcano."

A professor whose wisdom I greatly respect has a less dramatic explanation. He thinks that the attention span of those who are not deeply committed to any radical cause is not long enough to hold their interest. They simply get bored. The radical activist core, he says, hasn't changed; but they are not able to interest other students as much as they once did.

At one time, the radical leaders would have said, "Let's go burn the ROTC building!" and off they all would go—a few who didn't like ROTC on principle but hadn't thought of doing anything overt about it; a large number to whom ROTC smacked of Vietnam and the draft (but who also had had no thought of striking out physically against it); and then the biggest group who responded out of a youthful sense of excitement: this was something to do, and they had nothing better to do at the moment.

This last group, that always makes the difference between a gang and a mob, is the group that has gotten turned off. In part it is a matter of attention span, and in part it is a reaction to the excesses that inevitably revolted intelligent people.

As one of my young friends puts it, "We are tired of marching and disgusted with trashing."

So now, when the radical activist rings the gong, this group stays away. Where their attention has turned is less sharply defined, and this in itself is a symptom: instead of being polarized around a single set of issues, today their focus is much more diffused. This has disturbed some older students who have returned to the campus for graduate study after an absence of a few years.

I talked one day with a group of such students who had been undergraduates at Berkeley during the most turbulent days, had graduated, worked for periods of one to three years, then returned to the campus for graduate study. To a man—and woman—they were surprised and puzzled by what they found on the campus. Where was the activism? Where were the frenzied rallies? Where were the rabble-rousing speechmakers? In short, where was all the excitement? And was the concern gone, along with the excitement?

Each one had a slightly different answer, but they all agreed that things had changed.

After an hour of hot-and-heavy arguments as to why the change, there was a kind of consensus—no unanimity, but at least a majority view—that it was unrealistic to expect to find things exactly as they were before. Even as a matter of the attention span I have mentioned, people cannot stay stirred up indefinitely about the same things. Some individuals can, but large groups will either push on to some kind of action or lose interest, at least for a breathing-spell period. They may come back to it, but in the meantime they will let it simmer down for a while.

Furthermore, enough things had changed that a new crop of students, a totally new college generation, would not find the same things to protest that the previous crop had rebelled against. While not everything had been "corrected" in their eyes, some of the worst had been. Not only was U.S. growing involvement in Vietnam gone, and therefore the draft, but many age-old irritants in campus life were hardly recognizable.

In fact, some of the new freedoms were so new—and so free—that a young person recently transplanted from the restraints of life under the parental roof must have had difficulty finding any time or energy for protest.

In spite of the fact that some of my young companions of that morning were appalled that the current undergraduates were talking exactly like the students of the 1950s —pondering what they were going to do for a living, speculating on which field offered the most money, wondering about the job market—most of them were willing to accept a thesis that I tried out on them. It involves a principle that I find running through every field of human organization and social action. I call it "the base-line concept."

The freshman who entered the university in 1973, no matter how much he may have sounded like the freshman of 1953 (he certainly didn't look like him!), is not the same person. The moral issues, the political issues, the social issues,—in general, the values—that were barely discussed in the fifties and were battlegrounds in the sixties are now accepted as norms in the seventies. They are the floor, the platform, the baseline for the freshman of 1973–74. He may question any part of it—and over time there may be swings back from one or another part of it, as there always have been throughout history—but meanwhile he does not have to fight to defend these values as if they were his own special form of lunacy if he chooses to adopt them.

So what is there on the campus to be "activist" about, until he finds new injustices to correct?

Another perceptive friend of mine, once in the academic world and now heading a business complex that gives him unusual perspective on popular movements, describes this "base-line" phenomenon in a graphic way. He says that when the great swell of unrest on campuses and in the ghettos of our big cities reached crisis proportions, with the riots and burnings and bombings, it was like a river rising to flood stage and breaking over the banks. When it does, it cuts through new channels, and when the flood is over, the waters recede and the river subsides to a normal level—but it never goes back to the old channels.

He says that our turbulence has subsided and life goes on in a quieter mood, but make no mistake about it: it is flowing down different channels, and it will never be quite the same again.

My young friend, the college recruiter for industry, confirmed this thesis in his observations of the current crop of students. He finds them no less dedicated to the new cultural and social values than their predecessors were. Impressions I had gained from other sources would have prepared me for this, but his point of vantage gives a special validity to the view; and I find that he is not alone in it.

Many a corporate employer can testify that his young college recruits—even including his MBA's out of business schools—in the past few years are asking some different questions before they sign up to go to work. Along with the standard questions about pay and opportunity and challenging work there are questions about the company's social policies and about the opportunity for the young recruit to become involved in some aspect of social action.

Meanwhile, the more important question is whether the student concern and involvement of the late sixties and very early seventies has finished for *those* students of these years. Wherever they may be now, have they forgotten all about their earlier concerns? Are they so caught up in the rat race, the sports page or the *Wall Street Journal,* the TV at night, and the suburban lawn mowers on the weekend that social issues are just a memory of the past like *The Canterbury Tales?* The evidence is very much to the contrary.

They may be more relaxed, but considerable numbers of them are as earnest as ever.

The questioning of corporate management about social action does not stop at the employment interview. After they have been on the job a while, these bright, highly trained young minds bring up the questions again, and more pointedly as they begin to focus on company operations.

The new values that characterize the youth culture are by no means a monopoly of the young. For instance, while the young often talk as if they had discovered the environment as a problem, I am convinced that the real motive power, the real driving force, behind most environmental movements is coming from older people or, more accurately, from a coalition of all ages. Young people have a vital place in that picture—but they have lots of company. We probably never shall know to what extent the older people in the movement have been influenced by the younger, and vice versa. From my own experience I can testify that there has been a great deal of two-way indoctrination. It does not detract from the importance of that cross-pollination to say that of course there were effective, militant environmentalists (not always so labeled) long before the present youth were born. The concern of the young not only is needed to provide continuity, but comes at a peculiarly critical point in history.

In varying degrees, the same kind of bridge has been built between the generations in relation to many of the other values that have been newly embraced by so many of the young. We shall be looking at some of those values in the next chapter.

COUNTER CULTURE, YOUTH CULTURE, AND THE NEW VALUES

4

When we talk about the new value system that is emerging in America, what are we talking about?

The first time I can remember using those words out loud, the very conservative president of a very conservative college took issue with me even "out-louder."

"Do you mean to stand there and tell me that the Ten Commandments and the Golden Rule are now obsolete? Those are the values that I grew up with," he said.

I had to tell him that I hadn't exactly said what he had rhetorically put into my mouth. But he was "getting warm" in a sense that he did not suspect, because one of the basic premises of the new value system is: "I do not have to subscribe to anything just because *you* grew up with it." A corollary is that young people are likely to be turned off on almost *anything*—even something they might otherwise like—if it is handed to them with the understanding that "you must not question it."

We hear (and you will read here, now) several terms that sound like the same things and indeed are overlapping: Counter Culture, youth culture, new value system. While much has been written about the counter culture, it has not been precisely defined; and there have been no manifesto, no credo, and no party headquarters from which any such document could issue. Even less has been written in a definitive sense about the youth culture or the new value system.

So when I use the words here I shall tell you how I am using them. They are all fluid terms, because the things they represent are fluid—and not all flowing in the same direction. There are no sharp lines of demarcation but each has some identifying characteristics.

We can get the best perspective on the shifting values if we start by looking at the Counter Culture. While it has the fewest complete, outright adherents and probably has the least survival power, its attributes and its ideology as revealed in rock music and underground newspapers can be stated in the most clear-cut absolutes: it is anticompetitive; it reveres the present and has little interest in the future; it rejects the work ethic, in the sense of "work for work's sake," or as an evidence of good moral character; it rejects money and the material objects that money buys; it mistrusts reason and rationality, and places more trust in sensual awareness; it rejects the product of reason—technology; it views the corporation as an inhuman product of competition and technology which dehumanizes its members; it rejects authority and conformity wherever found.

It is plain that most of this credo is rejection, which is another form of protest or rebellion. It is a turning away from a whole pattern—and that pattern is what is variously called the Puritan or the Protestant Ethic. (I recognize that there are distinctions between the so-called Puritan and Protestant Ethics, but the line between the two is made fuzzy by the overlaps.) Virtually everything the Counter Culture accepts has its direct antithesis in that Ethic: The Protestant Ethic views competition as a testing ground of one's virtue and the Counter Culture considers competition a dehumanizing process which has made man fearful and suspicious of his fellow man—something basically evil that promotes exploitation instead of cooperation.

An important tenet of the Protestant Ethic is the belief in hard work. The seventeenth-century Puritan Cotton Mather instructed his congregation that "a man slothful in business is not a man serving the Lord." The Counter Culture claims that people work only for money and status, and since it rejects both money and status, it rejects work. This of course is the extreme position, because the Counter Culture is the extremist position. When I come, a little later, to the Youth Culture group, I shall refer again to the "work" issue; and then I shall hope to put it into broader perspective.

Benjamin Franklin is one of the favorite targets of the Counter Culture, because so many of his writings embodied the Protestant Ethic. Its concern for time is summed up in his essay "A Way to Wealth": "If time be of all things most precious, wasting time must be the greatest prodigality." Typical of the Counter Culture's reply to Franklin and the entire time concept is the song "Time" by the rock group Chicago:

> *Does anybody know what time it is?*
> *Does anybody really care?*
> *Who cares about time, about time?*

In the same article Franklin expressed the Puritan attitude toward savings and frugality:

> For age and want save while you may
> No morning sun lasts the whole day

The attitude of the Counter Culture was expressed by a rock group called Grassroots in their song "Live for Today":

> *Live for today, live for today*
> *Don't worry about tomorrow*

and by Allen Ginsberg, whose poem "Howl" is considered the founding document of the Counter Culture, when he wrote: "I have burnt all my money in a wastebasket."

The Counter Culture did not convert great masses to its particular life-style. As one of my young friends put it, only a relatively few persons actually "tuned in, turned on, and dropped out." Yet its strident message has compelled enough attention to cause those who come within earshot to question and reexamine their attitudes and values. Because the biggest exposure was among the young, the greatest rub-off was there; but there is ample evidence that many older people who may have scoffed at the absolutes of the Counter Culture still quietly "reviewed their own hand" and decided that some of their own absolutes could stand a bit of modifying.

For example, society has not chosen to ignore the time of day. People are not breaking their watches and throwing away their clocks. But people have begun to take a second look at the "rat race" and are no longer accepting it as an inevitable and inescapable fact of modern life.

None of the absolutes has been swallowed whole by any large segment of society, but each of them seems to have shaken substantial numbers of people of all ages loose from their rigid adherence to the absolutes at the opposite extreme.

We can see this most clearly among the youth, in what I have chosen to call the youth culture, just to identify and distinguish it from the extremism of the Counter Culture.

I have said earlier that it is hazardous to generalize about youth, and so I find the term youth culture a convenient device by which to identify the wide range of variation and difference within the student and other young age groups. Instead of having to clutter every sentence with qualifiers like "considerable numbers" or "many" or "there is a tendency" or "a trend," let me say categorically that whenever I refer to the youth culture I am talking about a phenomenon in which significantly large numbers of young people have adopted attitudes which differ significantly from traditional attitudes and which appear to be more than passing fads or poses. The numbers, percentages, and degrees of deviation will be different on every issue, but they are all substantial enough to foreshadow a real future impact on society.

One of the things that most sharply differentiates the youth culture group from the Counter camp is the very fact that it is not extremist, it is not absolute, it is not homogeneous, it is not 100 percent anything. It is all over the lot, on every count. The one thing it shares with the Counter Culture is that it does not buy the Protestant Ethic as a sacred, infallible, and absolute guide to all human activity. In fact, it would go further and say that nothing is so sacred and infallible that it should not be questioned before it is adopted as a rule of action for any given situation.

The youth culture expects to work, to earn money, to own material goods, but it rejects the work ethic as being the overriding imperative. It rejects the preocupation with business that it sees consuming the Standard American Male stereotype, but it does not reject business as having no place in its life. What it does particularly reject is the thought of ever becoming an "Organization Man."

If we say to the members of the youth culture, "Come in to our company . . . keep your head down . . . work hard . . . in thirty years you can be president or chairman of the board," they say the present-day version of "So what?" —or the four- and three-letter equivalent. They don't all know what they want—that's part of why they are confused—but they know they don't want that. They don't relish the prospect of becoming faceless persons, cogs in a great big machine.

The closest the youth culture comes to an absolute is its

rejection of the Great God Growth. It feels that the obsession with growth—which it sees as "Growth for Growth's Sake"—is the source of many of the other evils that it deplores. It sees this obsession in virtually every business; and when it sees economic growth as one of the three goals of national economic policy, it feels that even our national priorities have become twisted.

The emphasis on success, and on competition in every phase of life to test who is a success, particularly turns youth culture off. Achievement is fine; pride in excellence of performance is better; but competition—no.

In general, youth culture puts more weight on quality than on quantity: "Biggest Is Best" is an absurdity in Y.C. eyes. Because of this and several other convictions, it views our Market Economy as a Garbage Economy. It abhors the production of things for which there is no apparent need, and then the pressure of advertising and merchandising to create wants. It feels that the pressure to convert those wants into virtual needs has added an unnecessary measure of unsatisfied expectations that contributes to social unrest.

While goals and targets, in the sense of something that simply must be reached at the pain of being a failure, are not acceptable in the youth culture, a special scorn is reserved for the Establishment practice of giving economic goals the top priority. Youth culture does not deny the importance of economic factors and economic considerations; but it would give at least equal weight to cultural, educational, health, and other non-economic objectives.

The youth culture considers preoccupation with business to be part of what it calls "the plastic world"—a world it shuns. That attitude was dramatized—almost caricatured—in the motion picture The Graduate: The young man has returned home after graduating from college and is obviously going through the phase, so popular now, of "trying to find himself." A homecoming party is arranged in his honor by his parents who insensitively invite mostly guests of their own generation and "crowd." The graduate is turned off by everything he sees and hears at the party, and becomes even more withdrawn. Finally, one of the louder of the guests, an Old Family Friend who is also plainly the Success type, draws him off into a quiet corner where he is obviously going to share with him one of the great pieces of wisdom of all time. After glancing furtively around in all directions to make sure no one is overhearing him, he whispers to the boy, "I'm going to share with you the real key to the future." A dramatic pause. "Plastics!"

The anti-Establishment feeling of youth culture is a compound of many factors. In part it grows out of its revulsion against the Vietnam war and its disgust with everyone and everything that had a part in prolonging it. And government and business establishments are both charged with heavy guilt in that sphere. The war was a factor, but only one factor, in another kind of anti-Establishment development in the youth culture: a general erosion of confidence in our institutions. Business, government, church, university, the courts—all the institutions of our society to which people used to look up in respect—have lost their standing in these young eyes.

Whether as cause or as result, there is another expression of this anti-Establishment feeling on a highly personal level: the rejection of all externally imposed (in other words, institutional) discipline. This one has a more affirmative corollary: what is called "authenticity" in the youth culture, or "doing your own thing."

Both the negative and the affirmative sides of this value have been involved in the kicking off of traditional sexual restraints and the adoption of new (to this historical period) mores and practices.

Business Week magazine, at the time when campus unrest was at its most turbulent, published an article that sought to explain to its business readers how the current generation of students differed from campus dissidents of the past. What differentiates "post-modern youth," as *Business Week* called them, is their "life-style"—their approach to living and values. The elements of that life-style were classified differently in that article from the way I have classified them above, and some elements I have not previously touched were mentioned. But the views expressed in the article are generally consistent with my observations and give some additional insight and illumination.

The four major features of this new life-style singled out in this article are:

1. *Present-minded.* Students believe that how one lives today is more important than how one lives tomorrow. They are not goal-oriented and chide business for having goals. They are truly a *"now* generation."
2. *Personalism.* They seek open, honest relationships and fight what they term nonreciprocal personal ties. They flout convention to identify their individuality.
3. *Hedonism.* They live for pleasure and the most common expression of this is their desire for sexual freedom. They believe in "if not happiness, at least pleasure," a view that prompted one wag to comment, "To an activist student, chaste is waste." The Puritan culture is rejected by post-modern youth as well as the work ethic that is fundamental to it.

(While the article does not point this out, my own observations prompt me to stress again that it is not work itself that is rejected, but the glorifying of work as a great moral imperative—the so-called work ethic. Vast numbers of the young are tremendously hard-working, but they are more likely to be working for a purpose than just because someone has preached to them about the virtues of hard work.

It seems paradoxical that the young should reject so many elements of the Puritan ethic, including its views on work, and then embrace so many teachings of the Buddhists who revere work. But perhaps it is not as much of a paradox as it at first appears; because the

Buddhists esteem work for its humanizing values—not just its economic values alone. The Buddhist view would seem, to many of today's young, much more valid than the Puritan as a reason for working.)
4. *Involvement.* Post-modern youth believes that a decision is illegitimate unless the people affected by it participate in its making.

Whatever one may think of the particulars—and it is hard for anyone who has lived a half century or more not to believe that some of these will bring later disillusionment—the one thing that cannot be faulted is the honesty and openness of the approach.

The *Business Week* article goes on to observe that the post-modern youth sometimes appears arrogant, but that arrogance often masks a feeling of unsureness. I must confess that I hardly found that characteristic anything that distinguished post-modern youth from all the rest of us!

One other comment, however, I found worth repeating: "The post-modern youth comes off as idealistic, articulate, precocious, and sincere. He tends to argue with high-blown rhetoric, often memorized from polemics. His knowledge of history is thin or nonexistent."

One new value of the youth culture involves the concept of patriotism. What shook the traditional concepts was, again, a compound of many things, starting of course with Vietnam. The bitterness, frustration, and anger over that issue were such that the old flag-waving, breast-beating kind of patriotism did not have a chance to survive.

Then when the young began to feel that the same Establishment that was fostering the Vietnam engagement was also demanding conformity to the established social norms, demanding fealty to the "Bigger Is Better" and "Growth for Growth's Sake" credos, they began to think their country was sick. The fact that many self-appointed patriots accused the young of treason for even questioning the Establishment tenets did not help.

And yet these were not the radical extremists that were spreading "Hate America" poison. Many of them would have said—many did—that they loved their country more than their critics did: that they loved America enough that they wanted to save it, while their critics only wanted to exploit it.

"Patriotism" is an over-used, an exploited word, but in its best sense I think that there will be a resurgence of patriotism in some years—that we are in a pendulum swing and that the pendulum will, in time, swing back.

There may be pendulum swings in many of the symptoms of the youth culture, and this may be one of them. But they won't be quick swings. I doubt that two or three years will bring any sudden change and I doubt that the pendulum swing will bring any return to conventional expressions of patriotism.

It is my observation that history repeats itself, but never exactly. I expect young people in America to have a growing feeling of devotion to and affection for their country as they put their disenchantment over Vietnam further behind them; but I do not expect it to be the blindly unquestioning, or blatantly chip-on-the-shoulder, "my country, right or wrong" kind of patriotism. I expect it to be the kind of love a conscientious parent shows for his child.

There is an even more basic distinction involved here. The patriotism of our young, as I sense it, is tied to something very fundamental to the history of this country. The real thread of devotion that runs down through our two centuries of national life is not just a mystical love of the land—as we find in Russia—not just fealty to an authority system—as in earlier Germany; not just a pride in a "Jolly Good Empire"—as in nineteenth-century Great Britain—but rather a dedication to an idea and an ideal. And our revolution was not so much *against* a ruling group as it was *for* an ideal of freedom and openness in how we were to govern ourselves. The documents that formed the philosophical base for the work of the Founding Fathers are a heritage to us from such men as Tom Paine and Thomas Jefferson. The cluster of ideas embodied in those documents are at the core of the patriotism of today's youth.

Virtually all the new values that we now attribute to the young as part of the youth culture are beginning to show up in older circles. We shall probably never know how much of it was a rub-off from the young and how much was already there but never acknowledged until the young provided a more articulate and defensible rationale, but we do know that countless men and women argued with their young and then quietly said to themselves (and to each other), "You know, there's something in what they say. We *have* gotten ourselves into a rut and a rat race."

When Calvin Coolidge in 1925 said, "The business of America is business," a thoughtful people nodded, "Why, yes . . . that's right." Today's young people are saying, "That's not enough." Some are going further and saying, "Business is ruining America. Business is destroying our national resources, polluting our air and our water. Why? To produce garbage—things we don't need—and must throw away to keep the economy going. It's a garbage economy, and we don't need it."

The people who talk that way are not all young. An increasing number of older people are raising questions like that; and a few of them have been doing it for a long time. Twenty-five years ago, when I ran the chamber of commerce, there were thoughtful people who said, "You are ruining San Francisco and the Bay Area, bringing in industry and attracting more people." Now, in a few major cities, that kind of thinking is finding expression in organized movements: one started in Seattle, where the chamber of commerce is the Greater Seattle Chamber of Commerce—the new organization is called Lesser Seattle—and it is dedicated to keeping Seattle from growing.

Most of that thinking, even if it grew to the proportions

. of any kind of "movement," is aimed only at protecting
that area from growth. "Don't bring it here—take it somewhere else" is the theme song.

But there is a rising sentiment against growth per se—
the feeling that "bigger is better is bunk." The agitation for
Zero Population Growth is one expression of that feeling.

The rate at which older people can convert to new
values is in inverse ratio to their emotional commitment to
their traditional values and beliefs. The pain and trauma
involved in even facing that question will be examined in
the next chapter.

OLD ASSUMPTIONS CHALLENGED

5

If those of us who are older would like to learn some-thing from the whole period of campus upheaval and the growth of the youth culture, the first lesson is a tough one.

Lesson One is that we must be prepared to see all our assumptions—everything we have taken for granted all our lives—questioned and challenged. That is a painful ex-perience.

It is always painful to have doubt cast on a lifelong be-lief. Many of us can remember how traumatic it was in our freshman year in college to have courses in biology and psy-chology knock all the props out from under the religious beliefs we had brought to the campus. That can be so shak-ing an experience at that adolescent age that some youths of my time never quite got their bearings again.

One reason they became so unhinged and disoriented was that something vital was taken away from them, and no help given them to find something to take its place.

But young people are not the only ones who can be knocked off balance by having their values challenged. In fact, the older we get the more likely we are to hug our little prejudices and beliefs to our breasts because these are the sources of our security. When they are shaken, our security is shaken with them. And we are all too insecure anyway to be able to afford much erosion of our security.

Since the ones whose assumptions are being challenged now are not beginners in the world but the old-timers who have been around the track a few times, it is understandable that they would fight hard to defend their convictions—even to resist any questioning of them. They could feel even more desolate over the loss of a belief than a youth, because they would have less hope of finding anything acceptable, within their lifetimes, to take its place.

Will Rogers used to say, "Everyone is ignorant, but about different things." I would paraphrase that and say, "Everyone is insecure, but about different things." Most of us have a few areas in which we feel competent enough—either in some job skill, or some hobby area—that we feel secure there, but feel very unsure of ourselves everywhere else. More than that, many who know their jobs superbly well—and know that they know them—still are basically insecure as people. For all such, great comfort and security come from clinging to old familiar beliefs. This, I am sure, is why we do often hear clichés repeated with all the solemn authority of an oracle, typically, preceded by "I always say——": "I always say you shouldn't put all your eggs in one basket"; or, "I always say that a man who has never had to meet a payroll doesn't know anything about the problems of business."

And for all of us who are so insecure, a closed mind is our security blanket that we clutch like Linus in the "Peanuts" cartoons. But we had better be prepared to have that security blanket snatched away from us.

Being prepared to have our beliefs tested and questioned does not mean that we have to abandon or surrender them. We may be able to satisfy ourselves that we want to go on living with them even after we have looked at them in broad daylight. We may even be able to persuade others to accept them. But we won't be able to enjoy the luxury of telling young people that they should accept a philosophy just because we hold it, nor will we have the comfort of feeling that everyone holds the same view. We may find ourselves feeling a little lonely and deserted.

Shattering as this experience may seem at first blush, it need not destroy us. If our convictions cannot stand the light of examination, they are probably weak anyway and need more foundation support.

In a professional lifetime of counseling business managements on their corporate behavior, I have always counseled that every business should be prepared and willing to face the bar of public opinion every day of its life; that if it couldn't justify its existence to the public on a full disclosure of its facts, then sooner or later it was going to correct those facts or pay a penalty—possibly the penalty of the loss of its corporate life. The same principle applies to our personal convictions.

The doctrine of "Let there be heretics" was an early recognition of the mind-toughening value of having to stand up against dissent and attack.

Sometimes the heretics win the argument, though, and then we must be prepared to realize that things really are not exactly as we have been picturing them. We may find that we have let ourselves be trapped by our own semantics and especially by our slogans.

For example, we have used the phrase "The American Way of Life" as a banner to wave over every conceivable kind of cause. Yet, if we were to ask fifty people to tell us what "The American Way of Life" meant to them, we would get fifty different answers.

To some the answer would be in economic terms: freedom to invest, to make profits, to pursue any vocation. To others it might have philosophical or spiritual meaning: freedom of religion, freedom of expression. To still others, our competitive zeal to be first in everything—first in sports, first on the moon, first in Gross National Product—is the essence of the American Way.

All of this would be well and healthy, if the adherents of

each view didn't decide that theirs is the True Religion and try to impose it on everyone else. This approach lies at the very heart of the so-called generation gap, and it is a part of the cause of the decline in prestige of the modern corporation. Too many businessmen, many of whom are also fathers, have built up in their minds a stereotype image of the American Way which they often express in terms of "democracy." But they have lumped together a collection of values that have no necessary connection with democracy or with each other. They have equated democracy with free enterprise, economic growth, a market economy, competitiveness, being first in everything, patriotism, manliness, love of sports, and success—as if all were synonymous. Each of these values is of course subject to a wide range of interpretations.

We are surprised and hurt at times because other people bristle and recoil at words that to us have all the sanctity of home and motherhood. The term free enterprise is a good example. For most of my lifetime, those words have been accepted by the majority of our citizens as the very symbol of everything good: freedom was something we had often fought for, and enterprise was practically synonymous with productivity and fruitfulness. Only lately have we begun to listen to others carefully enough to realize that free enterprise means something quite different to many people in and out of this country. To them, it means unrestrained freedom to exploit.

Enterprise never has, in my lifetime, been as "free" as either of those interpretations would imply. People and their emotions polarized around words without thinking what they meant. A few things that we have held as sacred never were completely true; others were valid under earlier conditions, but no longer fit today.

You can't mount massive research and development (R&D) programs that challenge every physical law known to man and not expect the same questioning attitude to spill over into the social arena. We all grew up on the homely old saying, "You could no more do that than fly to the moon"—once the very ultimate measure of absurdity and impossibility. Now we have lost a handy piece of idiom, because somebody went and did it. But you can't go around doing things like flying to the moon and expect everything else to stay hitched right where it was. People are liable to start thinking.

And that is not necessarily bad, if we will really think and not just emote. If we are willing to go through the painful process of thinking instead of reacting defensively when some of our pet assumptions are challenged, then we will have the right to demand that our challengers do likewise—that they not use clichés and slogans as substitutes for thought. That is a human tendency.

Small wonder, in any case, that political, economic, social, and philosophical assumptions should now be challenged along with the physical. I say "challenged" rather than "disproven" because in the area of human behavior we may find that some of our most "old-fashioned" and "corny" concepts that are being most challenged actually stand up better under examination than do the doctrines of the physical sciences. I shall touch upon several of those in later chapters.

Today's young seem to be saying, in effect, what a young man in our bank said when told that he should be more deferential to the opinions of one of the older officers.

"After all," he was told, "Joe has had twenty years of experience on that job."

"Hell," said the youth, "Joe hasn't had twenty years' experience. He has had one year—repeated twenty times."

The desire of the young to stand on their own feet, to have ideas and values of their own, has been a wholesome development. But while I am often distressed by my business friends who close their minds against anything that departs from the cherished beliefs they have so carefully guarded and nurtured, I find myself growing equally impatient and amazed at the young who do the same thing. If there is any choice between the two, the odds should slightly favor the old, because change is so much more of a threat to them, and because their convictions and prejudices are based on such long-standing habit patterns. When young people announce that they are going to be "different," that they are going to "do their own thing," that they are not going to be chained to the conventions of their elders, and then begin to ostracize any of their contemporaries who do not dress as they do, who do not mouth the same tired, hackneyed phrases that stereotype them as "belonging," then I realize that the closed mind does not necessarily belong exclusively to any one age group.

There is a new game going on. Some hail the change as a great blessing, a great boon. More and more, though, the enthusiasm has been restrained, and a few critics view the process with such horror that they are sounding the bell of alarm for the future.

Alvin Toffler's brilliant book *Future Shock*, for example, turns the spotlight on our frantically accelerating pace of life and analyzes the disastrous consequences of that acceleration—both now and increasingly in the future. Toffler asks the right questions and cites the right dangers, but I quarrel with him on two major points:

One, in his basic premise: there seems to be an assumption of the *inevitability* of the runaway acceleration we now are experiencing. This is the assumption our economic pundits, our business forecasters, and our investment analysts have also made. Business plans and investment forecasts are universally predicated on the assumption of growth, and not only growth, but annually compounded growth, the so-called exponential growth. I think those who make such forecasts are due to have their own brand of future shock. They—and in this respect, Alvin Toffler—are wrong. It cannot be assumed that all lines on the charts will continue upward indefinitely.

There are natural forces, some of them beyond human control, and there are matters of decision, very much subject to human choice, both of which I see beginning to operate and both of which can have powerful influence over the future course of those growth trends. I shall touch on these in my chapter on the environment.

The possibility or probability of the slowing down of this pattern of acceleration does not minimize the urgency of learning to cope with it. Here is where I find my second major disagreement with Toffler.

The final section of *Future Shock* Toffler has devoted to "Strategies for Survival." With most of his strategies I can agree; the closer he stays to the individual and what he can do to help himself, either entirely by himself or in closely related groupings, the more I can applaud his prescriptions. Even his chapter on "Education in the Future Tense" I found profoundly thoughtful and constructive, even though I shall argue elsewhere in this book with one point he makes there.

It is his final chapter that gives me difficulty. Entitled "The Strategy of Social Futurism," it must represent his ultimate solution, for he not only reserves for it the climactic spot in the book but builds within it toward what is obviously his crowning conclusion: that our planning for the future must be done by "a revolution in the production of utopias: collaborative utopianism. We need to construct 'utopia factories.' "

He suggests that we "assemble a small group of top social scientists—an economist, a sociologist, an anthropologist, and so on—asking them to work together, even live together, long enough to hammer out among themselves a set of well-defined values on which they believe a truly superindustrial utopian society might be based."

He would create a great international institute of the future, which "would take as its purpose the collection and systematic integration of predictive reports generated by scholars and imaginative thinkers in all the intellectual disciplines all over the world: . . . Attempts to bring this knowledge together would constitute one of the crowning intellectual efforts in history—and one of the most worthwhile."

He decries—as he should—the elitism of the technocrats, but he somehow fails to see in his proposals an equivalent elitism of the intellectual and the academic.

Because he says he wants to avoid the elitist approach in the final decision-making, he proposes that each of the high-technology nations of the world literally set aside the next five years as a period of intense national appraisal; at the end of five years to come forward with its own agenda for the future, a program embracing not merely economic targets but broad sets of social goals.

To implement this, he would convene in each nation, in each city, in each neighborhood, "social future assemblies" to represent not merely geographic localities, but social units —industry, labor, the churches, the intellectual community, the arts, women, ethnic and religious groups, students, "with organized representation for the unorganized as well."

Earlier in the chapter he deplored the lack of nationally integrated goals to bring order out of chaos, and stated that "the absence of coherent policy is equally marked and doubly dangerous." He then cites the unsuccessful efforts of Presidents Eisenhower, Johnson, and Nixon to have such coordinated goals policies formulated and made effective, whether developed through blue-ribbon commissions, through Cabinet departments, or through special White House staffs.

The "participative democracy" that is implied in Toffler's proposal is commendable, but when addressed to as complex a body of abstractions as the shape of the future, it is naïvely unrealistic. Anyone who has worked with "community forum" types of movements knows how difficult it is to reach agreement on *anything* in such a setting. Those of us who helped to bring the Urban Coalition into being after the Watts, Detroit, and other riots in 1964 had in front of us a real laboratory model of what I am talking about: we had exactly the pattern of representation that Toffler proposes; and while the task to which we were to address ourselves—to mobilize the resources of our community in an effort to solve the problems of the "Inner City" (the ghetto)—was complex enough, it was ABC-simple compared with Toffler's assignment to the future social assemblies. Yet this became one of the most frustrating exercises in futility of my lifetime.

Instead of addressing itself to action on specific problems, which many of the most dedicated leaders tried earnestly to do, the Coalition in Los Angeles became a perennial debating society. I gather that other large cities had a similar experience. Six years after our founding, when my retirement compelled me also to drop out of the Coalition, we were still debating over how we were to be organized: how much representation was to be given to each of the minorities (primarily black and Mexican-American), how much prominence was to be given to these same groups in the officerships, how the policies were to be worded, how the bylaws were to be worded, etc., etc. I am told by my successors that some of this is still going on, although after eight years some real progress has been made.

I must add, with no rancor or bitterness, that the representatives of the minorities, who were intended to be the beneficiaries of all the Coalition efforts, were anything but easy to deal with. It is possible that the businessmen on the Coalition board and committees may have had too much of a "Lady Bountiful" approach; they may have been condescending or patronizing—but I don't think so. Obviously I am a prejudiced witness, and I may have been one of the worst offenders, but my feeling throughout this effort was that the blacks and Chicanos had chips on their shoulders, as if they resented the "big shots" who were coming in to tell the ghetto residents how things should be fixed up.

There was an implied attitude (often more openly expressed than implied) that if the fat cats from downtown would just provide the money and then stay away everyone would be much happier.

Month after month, the business leaders would leave these meetings feeling so frustrated that they would want to say "to hell with it" and quit. But month after month they would go back and try again.

I recite all this history not as any indictment of the Urban Coalition: I think that the very difficulty of making it work only demonstrates how crucially important it is that it, or something like it, be *made* to work. The gulf in communications is tremendous, in spite of all the dedicated efforts of fine people on both sides of the gulf; bridging that gulf is mission enough to justify a Coalition, because bridging that gulf is imperative if the gulf is not to deepen and split us off into two warring worlds.

(Parenthetically, I think we will make more progress in building that bridge when we respect each other's maturity enough to speak plainly about these issues instead of tiptoeing around in fear of hurting tender feelings. Obviously, none of us—blacks, Chicanos, or whites—had enough know-how in this strange new venture of dealing with each other to know how we should go about it.)

The reason I spell all this out is to illustrate how futile I think it is to expect forums to reach conclusions on abstract issues soon enough to have any significant effect on the problems of the future. The difficulties of reaching agreement in any one community would be multiplied logarithmically as we moved to national and international arenas.

I do not belittle the desirability of encouraging the kinds of discussion that Toffler envisions. At worst, it would help to sharpen the awareness that the future is multidimensional. I say only that the decisions and the actions that must be taken to cope with the future will not come out of such debating societies as his assemblies would become.

The decisions and the actions will come, as most decisions and actions throughout history have come, one at a time, a piece at a time, on one problem at a time. Particularly in a democracy but to a considerable degree under even the most absolute of autocracies, the pattern of a society is built up, bit by bit, as a composite of many separate actions. The complexion of those actions—conservative or radical, pacifist or belligerent, nationalistic or international, secular or ecclesiastic—will be colored by the attitudes of those who hold the power, whether populace or ruler; but those attitudes will be effectively expressed in one action at a time.

In any case, most of us are going to have to make our peace with this fast-changing world by ourselves as individuals. Whether or not we become part of any larger movement that is attempting to deal with the great issues, each of us as an individual will have to make his own accommodation to the fact of change.

The first step in facing it is to recognize that the world around us is a moving target, and always has been; that the "status" doesn't stay "quo" very long, and never has. There is an old wheeze to the effect that Adam said to Eve, as they were leaving the Garden of Eden, "Darling, we are living in a time of transition." The only difference between that time of transition and this one is that the transiting is happening so much faster. In more elegant language, the rate of change is accelerating.

The second step is to recognize that when change comes so fast, there is no reason to consider the new pattern any more permanent than the old one that it replaces. It too will be replaced by something newer.

This is hard on those who get their security from a sense of permanence, and we all do to some degree. Child psychologists have found that children need a predictable world, consistency, and a certain amount of routine; when these elements are absent they become anxious and insecure. To the degree that adults are immature—and most of us are, in some respects—we have the same needs. But that dictates that we look to a different source for our permanence. The externals and the physical trappings of living never have been very permanent; styles and fashions have been even less so. Modes of transportation are the most dramatic example, when we can see the change in one lifetime from the horse and buggy to the primitive "Model T" to the high-speed, high-powered luxury car; and from the passenger train to the small piston-engine airplane to the jet and now to the supersonic jet (heaven forbid!), with the trolley streetcar appearing and disappearing again in favor of the bus.

Millions of people have seen the rotating exhibit of General Electric at the New York World's Fair or at Disneyland, in which a typical American family is shown in the setting of several stages of the modernization of a home: first with the old wood stove, the kerosene lamp, and the long-handled pump pumping water out of the well into the kitchen; then the crude early electrification, with light cords dangling from the ceiling, bare electric light bulbs, and a spaghetti of extension cords to primitive electric appliances; then the more modern and more streamlined appliances; and finally the sophisticated contemporary home with the electrical equipment more subtly tucked away. I have not talked with anyone who saw that exhibit who did not say that his choice would have been at least one stage earlier than the last one shown in the exhibit: it was convenient and it was elegant, but it was *sterile*. There was no warmth, no suggestion that it really was being lived in.

The General Electric team that designed these rooms undoubtedly never suspected that they were doing something that undermined the message they were trying to convey, but somehow they had managed to make the husband and wife in the earlier versions look happier than their counterparts in the slick modern home!

The nostalgia that led so many people to react in that way, and to look longingly at the reminders of "the good old days," may be, with most of them, a form of wishful thinking that will not find expression in action.

But this reaction isn't all looking backward. Much of it is involved with making present and future choices. Many values don't depend on material goods. They depend on relations and interaction with other people, or on interaction with things in nature. In many of those relationships, what we call material comforts actually get in the way.

Anyone who has gone on pack trips, or to a mountain cabin, knows that some of the most memorable moments have been the conversations while cooking, building fires or scrubbing dirty pans; it was the flow between two or more persons that was rewarding. Not only does that not depend on comforts or luxuries but it often seems to thrive best in the elemental setting.

I am not suggesting that everyone was happier when everyone had less; nor am I using that premise as an argument for scaling down our economy and our per capita consumption of goods. What I am saying is that possessions have made little difference, one way or the other. There have always been people who could find great joy in their lives without much material wealth, and their kind will usually—but not always—find joy when surrounded by more material affluence. There are others who are always miserable when they have nothing. Their type also is likely to be miserable even when they have material comforts and luxuries, especially if others have even more than they.

There is much to be said for modern conveniences and for the modern technology that makes physical things so plentiful. But the central point to remember is that those things, of and by themselves, have little or nothing to do with the satisfactions life has to offer. Those satisfactions, other than those of satisfying the most basic physiological needs, come from activities that do not depend upon physical equipment. What Dr. Abraham Maslow, in his famed

Hierarchy of Needs, has identified as the "growth needs" involve relations with others or relations with oneself, but not relations with things.

So in a high-speed, high-technology world where *things* proliferate and complicate—then evaporate—we can look at them with amused detachment, pick and choose the ones we want, ignore the ones we don't—and not be bullied by them.

(As Maslow made plain, a person who lacks even the barest necessities for physical survival—and there are millions of such persons—can have little interest in gratifying any higher needs. The awareness of this tragic disparity is in itself a strong motivating factor in the reexamination, even by many whose basic needs are being amply satisfied, of the priorities that we have given to our social and economic uses of our energies.)

This picking-and-choosing process is closely akin to another and more basic decision. We can call this one Step Number Three: the decision that we do not have to accept all change without challenge.

Make no mistake about it: if we set out to resist change, we will have battles—some difficult ones. We will have some defeats and some disappointments. It is likely that the change we oppose is somebody else's pet project, and he will never forgive us for trying to obstruct it.

So—the fourth step—we have to decide what we think is worth fighting for—or fighting about. It dictates that we reexamine our own values and decide what we think is important. It becomes a time of sorting out; a time of separating the permanent values from the passing fancies; a time of judging which of our values are based only on the customs and fashions of our town or our crowd or our generation, and which are based on what we believe is the wisdom of the ages; a time of sifting out the substance from the trifles.

At such a time as that, we would quickly see that the

length of a man's hair or of a woman's skirt, or whether he wears a beard or they both wear beads—that these are trifles; but what happens to a stream or a lake or the air we breathe—these are not trifles. Whether people worship in a church or in a synagogue or on a hillside, whether they kneel or sprinkle water on each other, whether their skins are white, yellow, red, brown or black—these are all trifles; but if any one is denied equal opportunity because of one of these differences—or demands special treatment because of the difference—these are not trifles.

The fifth step is a decision, too: the decision not to get high blood pressure over the trifles. I happen to think that high blood pressure is not the most effective approach to *any* project—someone has said that it is no solution to a problem to get apoplexy in the face of it—but it is amazing how often we use our biggest doses of adrenaline on our most trivial problems. We should save it for the big ones, and even then to keep our poise and our flexibility, remembering that when any adversary goes rigid he is a sitting duck for attack.

There are many reasons for urging the counsel of poise, which is relaxed strength. Only a few of the reasons are related to the tactics of winning the immediate engagement; the others are related to living with our adversaries when this contest is over. We have to risk making enemies at times, but in building a society, the weakest piece of lumber is a chip on the shoulder.

THE LESSONS OF HISTORY

6

In the months following the burning of the bank at Isla Vista, I became increasingly aware that we in business and we who were older had a great deal to learn about our young people. But I also became painfully aware that those young had a lot to learn, too, and I found myself repeating over and over the words of George Santayana: "Those who cannot remember the past are condemned to repeat it."

I felt that particularly keenly when I would talk with the real revolutionaries—those who acknowledged that they wanted to destroy the present system and start over. I felt sure that they were headed for the most tragic disillusionment, particularly if their revolution were successful.

History suggests that a new power structure of bully boys would soon take over and that true liberalism would be the first thing to be liquidated.

Even after the violence had cooled and most of my contact was with those who were talking only about "change within the system," I felt some of this same concern about the potential disillusionment of the more militant of the young people—not because they wanted change but because I felt they were unrealistic about how it could be brought about. They were on the scent of the right problems, the things that need correcting, but what they wanted to do ignored the lessons they should have learned from history.

What they believed—and what history shows to be a vain hope—was that all the problems of society could be solved by one great stroke:

—one great piece of legislation

—one drastic reorganization of our whole corporate business structure

—or one revolutionary reshuffling of government and society.

A lesson that may not yet be apparent to the young—or to their elders—is that the reforms they seek will never be achieved in one single stroke.

Many evils have been corrected by revolution, to be sure, but only when, as in our American Revolution, there was built into the revolutionary process the machinery for constant renewal and maintenance of the correction process. For one of the most basic of human truths is that nothing stays fixed for very long.

A corollary is that really big problems rarely are completely fixed even for one moment of time. Our Civil War eliminated the institution of slavery in this country but it made little provision for adapting and assimilating the former slaves into a society for which they had not been prepared; a century later we are still wrestling with by-products of that transition.

We can create a perfect house or a perfect office building for a week or two, until we begin to create problems by our occupancy. Anyone who ever has built either a house or an office building will testify that the problems really begin after move-in.

Human organizations and their operations are never perfect and never complete. They are fluid, changeable, and in constant need of adjustment. This poses the most challenging problems of a democracy:

—to stay hitched to the never-ending, often-boring routine
of keeping our human institutions "tuned up" and "relevant";
—above all, to keep people excited about it.

It is much more exciting and exhilarating to tear something down and put something new in its place. It is much
more fun to plant a garden than it is to cultivate it, weed it,
and water it. It is more stimulating to build and create almost anything than it is to have to maintain it.

The same principle operates for those who would reform
our government or any other part of our society. The
planting, cultivating, and weeding are endless: good innovative ideas can be planted in the public consciousness,
but unless support for the ideas is cultivated over a long
period of time, interest and attention will lag before the
idea can ever be put into action. The weeding takes the
form of endless vigilance, lest a good original idea be distorted and bastardized, whether by its enemies or by its misguided friends. That kind of sabotage can happen at any
time along the line, from the time the idea is first brought
out for discussion until long after it is fully operative as a
going project.

The perils of the reform trail were spotlighted during the
days of the Depression in California when it was realized
that the social welfare machinery of the state and the counties was not adequately designed for the mounting problems that faced the state. A coalition of organizations with
widely differing views on most subjects, including the state
chamber of commerce and the League of Women Voters,
joined forces to back a highly successful legislative program
that revamped structures and procedures so thoroughly that
it was hailed as a real reform achievement. Having accom-
plished its mission, the coalition dissolved and there was no
one left with both the interest and the muscle to make sure
that the new setup was not tampered with. The inevitable

happened: political forces chipped away at the program to such an extent that, five years after, it was hardly recognizable.

So reform is a little like love and marriage: the excitement and drama of a revolutionary coup, like the romance of a whirlwind courtship, are all well and good, but it is what happens during the long tedious period of dishwashing and bedmaking that tests how good the marriage is.

I have twice in my life worked in a company where the founder was a great creator and builder but had neither the patience nor the skill to operate it smoothly once it was built. Fortunately in both cases the founder was followed by a man who might never have been able to create the organization but was able to consolidate and operate it successfully. (Neither of these, incidentally, was the Bank of America, where the founder developed good men as he went along. But even there, the transition from the intuitive operation of a creative founder to the professional management that by then was imperative was blessed by a providentially fortunate chain of succession.)

Whether it be a garden, or an agency of government, the payoff comes in maintaining, cultivating—if necessary, pruning and weeding—so that it yields the full production for which it was designed.

DEVILS AND HEROES

7

Because we have a human tendency to want to find "devils" for everything we don't like—to look for someone to blame whenever things are not to our liking—many young people have come to regard "the System" or "the Establishment" or "the Corporations" as some kind of conspiracy, a group of people who have deliberately connived to create the conditions the young now deplore.

Without either defending or apologizing for all the end results, I have tried to put our economic history into perspective for the young people with whom I have talked. I think this backward glance is a useful exercise for the rest of us if we want to understand the terms of the debate we are engaged in.

For thousands of years the struggle for just the bare necessities has dominated men's lives. Then, all of a sudden, within a century-plus, and, more dramatically for the citizens of the "have" nations, within one lifetime have come the technological breakthroughs that have changed all that. It was not surprising that we should all get swept up in the excitement of producing—and in the excitement of the whole game of producing things. Because there had been such need, here and all over the world, production had become the goal, and those who could produce were heroes. Small wonder that there was little thought of what else was happening: if people needed lumber for houses, you cut down trees; and if you needed tractors to get the lumber out, you built factories to build the tractors; and if you needed fuel, you drilled oil wells and built refineries; and you used whatever land was needed, and did whatever you had to do to that land. You not only weren't deliberately doing anything bad, you not only were doing what had to be done, but you felt quite virtuous about it—you were a great achiever. In fact, throughout most of history, the concept was that it was a struggle of man against nature; man was trying to conquer nature and the elements, to harness them; so as man acquired mechanical means to do that, he had quite naturally a great sense of triumph.

Now we wake up to realize that in the process of "conquering" nature, we were in fact destroying it and destroying part of our own lives with it.

But it was natural that business should be drawn along on its own momentum and be so caught up in the game of production that production would become an end in itself. Having set out originally to meet "needs," it now must create "wants" for the things it produces; and it has been this very transition that has generated a large part of the flak—the resentment and criticism of the ecological damage and destruction of natural resources that are laid at the door of the corporate business.

Ralph Lapp, in *The New Priesthood*, was writing about where science was taking us, but he could just as well have been talking about the economy when he said, "We are aboard a train which is gathering speed, racing down a track on which there are an unknown number of switches leading to unknown destinations. No single scientist is in the engine cab and there may be demons at the switch. Most of society is in the caboose looking backward."

If we want to make any headway on the problems of society in which business is involved, we will neither deify nor villify business or its corporations as a class but we will put them into proper perspective. They evolved and developed as a means of serving people's needs; we have been passing through an era in which business and economic goals have been so dominant in our lives that we had begun to act as if *people* should be serving *business'* needs. We are now emerging into another era in which the corporate person and the animate person should be working together to fill a new order and higher level of human needs.

Our needs are of an infinitely more complex nature than those we faced during the first two centuries of this nation's history and the Industrial Revolution. Because the solutions, consequently, will of necessity be vastly more complex than the simple job of producing things, they will need participation and cooperation from many segments of society that are not in the habit of working with each other— some of them not in the habit of working on public issues, period.

We hear a lot of clamor and demand that corporations assume a more active role for the good of society. But unless this clamor can be considered a social contribution (which in some cases it is), at least a few of the social critics would have to be classed as kibitzers, whose own records of constructive work for social good are not nearly as good as that of the companies or executives they criticize.

The moral of this observation is not that the critics should be silenced, No. The moral is, to repeat an old Indian expression we used to hear in Montana: "No man should criticize another until he has walked a mile in the other man's moccasins." In other words, he should have taken his own turn at doing something socially constructive before he has earned the right to criticize others' efforts.

The great bulk of what needs to be done to improve the lot of our people is going to need tremendous amounts of collaboration and cooperative effort among widely diverse elements in our society. It *can* be done, perhaps, in an atmosphere of bitterness, antagonism, and hostility such as is generated by constant name-calling; but it will be done twice as fast in the setting of "Come on, fellows, let's get this done" than it will to the chorus of "Why don't you blood-sucking robbers do it?"

WHOSE BUSINESS
IS SOCIETY?

8

I have spent most of my adult life in the orbit of the business corporation. I thoroughly believe in the corporate form of organization as the most effective instrument ever devised for mobilizing resources to meet human economic needs. I admire tremendously both the direct economic achievements and the many indirect, socially productive by-products of our corporate history.

At the same time, one would be blind if he did not recognize that out of the very achievements and flowering of this great productive mechanism have grown problems— all of them ultimately human problems.

Corporations themselves are going through a wave of soul-searching and self-examination as to their role in society and their degree of social responsibility. In discussing it here, I am going to put on my corporate hat again and address myself largely to my fellow business executives.

I had thought that business—the corporate management of business—had decided a generation or more ago that maximizing profits was not the *sole* concern of a corporation. A lot of other corporate managers had thought the same thing, had, in fact, taken it for granted and had simply gone on from there to do what they felt was right, without much philosophizing about "social responsibility" or "corporate priorities" or the other terms that later became issues of debate.

But then a number of forces came into play, all within a short span of time, that created doubts, uncertainties, and a high degree of confusion.

The publication of Rachel Carson's *Silent Spring* in 1962 and the appearance of Ralph Nader on the national scene in 1965, with the publication of his book *Unsafe at Any Speed*, might be taken as the first major, visible incidents that ushered in the new era. The organization structure that he created, with four umbrella organizations centrally directing research and action programs and state groups (in twenty-seven states at the time this is written) carrying this activity down to the state and local level, is clearly the largest and most extensively organized of the bodies engaged in the investigating of abuses against the consumer and the environment. But along with the Nader complex there have grown up more than a dozen other major activist groups turning the spotlight nationally on corporate social performance. The Council on Economic Priorities, the Project on Corporate Responsibility, and the Center for New Corporate Priorities are but a few of the movements that have come into being during this period; their titles are indicative of their purposes.

Then, in 1970, Dr. Milton Friedman, a professor of economics at the University of Chicago, took issue with this entire drift of events. In a widely publicized article in *The New York Times Magazine*, he propounded his thesis that "the social responsibility of business is to increase its profits." He particularly took to task those businessmen who even talked about the social responsibility of business, saying that they were unwitting puppets of intellectual forces that were undermining the basis of a free society.

With this, the fat was in the fire. The debates that followed Friedman's article were carried into the councils of business, onto campuses, and, occasionally, into the halls of government.

The criticism, defense, counterattack, and rhetoric that followed, often obscured the real issues more than they clarified them. It is useful now to endeavor to put the issues back into perspective, because debate along the lines drawn by Friedman misses the point entirely.

It is not a question of whether the good of society is the "prime" goal of business, or whether making profit is its "sole" objective. The good of society should be the primary goal of everyone in the society.

Of course each company has to make a profit to stay in business; so *of course* profit can be its "prime" objective without diminishing the emphasis given to other goals. In that sense, making profits is the primary objective of the business corporation, just as practicing medicine is the primary objective of the doctor; but it is profit maximization over the long term, not the short term.

It is obvious that if a company did not make a profit, it would not be able to do any of the other things it is called upon to do. And it is obvious that if it were not for the hope and expectation of a profit, the corporation would not have come into being in the first place. Corporations do not create themselves. They are created by people who choose to risk their savings, their capital, in the hope that they may thereby increase it.

Because these basics are so obvious, they would not be worth repeating except for the fact that in the current rhetoric over corporate social responsibility they often seem to be ignored or disputed.

So profit-making, of course, is the *primary* objective of a corporation; but that does not suggest that a company cannot have other objectives. The doctor practices medicine and the lawyer practices law; these may be their primary objectives in life, but that does not keep them from having many other objectives and interests. The professional person usually wants to be a good citizen; any decent human being wants to fulfill the obligations owed to family and friends; people may have hobbies they pursue with part of their time. None of these other objectives and interests need interfere with being an effective professional person, provided they are kept in reasonable balance. Any man or woman who is a good money manager sets priorities on what is to be done, and allocates time, energy, and resources on a rational basis.

Properly managed, these outside interests not only do not interfere with his professional career, but may even enhance and enrich it. They broaden his contacts, his insights, and his horizons generally, and they help to build his reputation in his community.

And so it is with the corporate person—the business firm. It may involve itself in a wide range of activities that have no visible connection with the business of making and selling things for a profit, and it can carry on those activities without taking its eye off the main target of its profit-making.

Many of these social activities are, indeed, of immediate self-interest; a retailer, for example, cannot long prosper in a community where unemployment is choking off purchasing power, or in a community where crime, violence, and delinquency are making people afraid to remain there, or in a community where air pollution makes it unpalatable to live there.

Sometimes the self-interest is there, but not so apparent; we call it "enlightened self-interest" when it is a degree more remote. This could apply to the manufacturer who has nothing to sell in the community, but wants to be able to attract and hold good personnel and so wants to keep the community a desirable place to live. It is still enlightened self-interest to help minorities achieve a more productive, effective place in society; educating, training, and preparing them for employment at higher levels of skills not only broadens our pools of available talent, but increases purchasing power and so expands the market for the sale of our goods and services. The same case can be made for the entire area of aid to education at all levels.

And in varying degrees the same case can be made for corporate support to a wide range of cultural and other activities that go beyond these areas and directly or indirectly better the quality of life.

Those are the optional things, the things the corporation does voluntarily, and that probably contribute to its own profitability, short-term or long-term. That is good; the conjunction of self-interests is one of the better routes to the happy society.

But business no longer has the choice, the privilege to the degree that it once had it, to stop at those optional programs that are carried on with one eye on its own self-interest. Those in corporate life are going to be expected to do things for the good of society, just to earn their franchise, their corporate right to exist. That is why I am both amused and amazed that there should even be a question about the *propriety* of corporate social involvement, when it is to me so clearly an *obligation*. The corporation has to earn its right to exist and to function—and it has to earn that right all over again every single day of its life. That is what we mean when we refer to "franchise": it is not a fixed, vested property; it is not a guaranteed right. It is a privilege that can be given—has been given—and can be taken away.

Those who spend their lives in the business arena are inclined to take that arena for granted, to think that they own it and are entitled to dictate all the rules of all the games that are played in it. They ought to know better, because they haven't played under a rule of their own for so long that hardly anyone alive today can even remember it!

To earn its franchise, the corporation is expected to do the right things on at least three levels:

1. At the first and most basic level, to produce and deliver its product or its service at a quality and at a price that the market will find acceptable.
2. Then, to carry on its own operations in a way that is fair to its employees, to its customers, and to its suppliers and that is not damaging in any way to the environment in which it operates.
3. And, finally, to be aware of the problems of the total community and of the total society and to do its share toward solving them.

Some of us can remember that the doctrine of "let the buyer beware" still ruled during our childhood. But within our lifetime the buyer has joined forces with other buyers and has decided to beware collectively. What we now call consumerism is not new but is an extension of a principle that goes back to the enactment of pure food and drug laws, weights and measures acts, and other decisions that products and services should be what they claim to be.

So at the basic level, the public's expectations from business are already pretty well undergirded by laws—laws that we can expect to see updated wherever performance falls short of promise.

At the middle level, most of us have lived through the full cycle as public attitudes have translated themselves into laws and regulations in labor relations, in trade practices, and now in environmental conditions. The early part of this century was still pretty largely *laissez-faire* in all those areas, but mid-century, starting with the legislation of the early thirties, saw a giant swing in the public temper to bring all those areas of human relations and behavior under control of the law.

But everything the public asked of business at the first two levels was simple compared with what will be expected at the third. Consumer concerns and even the regulatory confrontations were relatively "transactional" compared with the broad, deep problems that are now concerning society. It is not surprising that business is looked to for help at this third level because business has played so large a role in the history that brought these problems into being.

Notice that I do not say that business is "responsible" or "to blame" for these problems. I see little profit in the popular game of finding someone to blame for all problems. But I do see value for everyone in putting this current era into the perspective of history.

If we omit the Vietnam war, most of the other problems plaguing our society are the end result of a history that started with the Industrial Revolution, accelerated gradually into World War II, and then exploded with the Technology Revolution of post-World War II. All in one lifetime, we have gone from a semi-industrialized to an industrialized to a computerized economy; from the employment of unskilled to semiskilled and now to highly skilled workers. But perhaps the greatest change for all of us has come in the shift from a rural to an urban society.

When we generalize our current social problems under the umbrella phrase of "the urban problem," it is more than just a convenient euphemism. All the human problems that can come from crowding together too closely in big cities are summed up in that one phrase.

That is why I say that business has played a large role in that history. While no one in business ever willed it to be so, and probably no single individual in or out of business ever visualized the exact shape of things as they are today, the thing we call "Business"—the whole business process of producing, buying, selling, investing—has been the mechanism through which the Industrial Revolution and Technological Revolution have transformed us from the kind of society we were to the kind we are today. A writer for the *Economist* of London explained our present situation very well: "We have learned to cope superbly with the environment God created for us," he said, "but not with the environment we have created for ourselves."

So, along with the marvels and miracles of which we boast, we have to acknowledge that the transformation of our society has brought with it some social by-products that are not so welcome.

And what society is saying to business, in effect, is, "If you want the privilege of going on running this big, all-embracing, all-engulfing machine, you've got to help see to it that it produces a better quality of life for every-body."

Corporations, in the final analysis, exist by public consent—by public franchise. Therefore, the corporation has no choice but to engage in socially oriented efforts as a matter of earning its franchise, as a matter of self-preservation, and as a matter of obligation to do its share of the world's necessary work.

In a very basic sense it is the right of corporations to exist and to operate that is at stake today. And since it is rather important to exist if you want to make profits, even *this* reason for social involvement is not completely divorced from the profit motive!

There are two ways to go: business can look the other way, and wait for government to dictate all the answers as it has done on the two other levels that I have discussed; or it can pitch in and help to find the answers. Apart from the fact that the private sector, including corporate business, might do a better job on the particulars of the problem, there is another consideration that to me is over-riding, one that goes to the very heart of what kind of society we are going to have. If today's social problems are solved entirely by government, the rules imposed will be no mere transactional ordinances. They could take us a long step toward a monolithic society.

THE PLURALISTIC SOCIETY

9

America was once called a melting pot, and in a sense it was and still is; but I have preferred to think of us rather as a great mosaic in which our national character was not melted down into a monochrome but was built up bit by bit from the diverse characters, personalities, and contributions of millions of differing individuals into one brilliantly colorful whole.

To preserve and foster that pluralistic character requires the continued social involvement of the private sector, and it is significant that not all the resistance to that involvement comes from *laissez-faire* captains of industry or right-of-center economists. There are those—not in tremendous numbers, but strategically placed in government and in academic circles—who contend that social problems and concern for the public well-being should be the exclusive province of government, and that no one else should even be allowed to have a voice or a place in that field. They would propose, for example, that contributions to higher education not be deductible for tax purposes on the ground that the corporate or other private donor should not be allowed to influence, at the expense of other taxpayers, the course of education, which should be entirely in the control of government as the voice of all the people.

I prefer to place myself in the camp of Dr. James A. Perkins, who has said: "If we ever come to the point where it is widely believed that only those on the public payroll can work in the public interest, our free society will be doomed."

In the final reckoning, solutions to social, economic, and political problems are going to depend upon human judgment, human wisdom. The net, cumulative effect of a myriad of human actions and human decisions by fallible, frail human beings is what our society is, and all it ever can be. One does not suddenly become endowed with greater wisdom or keener judgment when one becomes part of government. And I think those of us outside government—particularly those who have special knowledge or expertise—have an equally valuable contribution to make.

Walter Lippmann expressed the case for pluralism very graphically in his little paragraph about the planner's breakfast. He wrote:

> The thinker, as he sits in his study drawing his plans for the direction of society, will do no thinking if his breakfast has not been produced for him by a social process which is beyond his detailed comprehension. He knows that his breakfast depends upon workers on the coffee plantations of Brazil, the citrus groves of Florida, the sugar fields of Cuba, the wheat farms of the Dakotas, the dairies of New York; that it has been assembled by ships, railroads, and trucks, has been cooked with coal from Pennsylvania in utensils made of aluminum, china, steel, and glass. But the intricacy of one breakfast, if every process that brought it to the table had deliberately to be planned, would be beyond the understanding of any mind. Only because he can count upon an infinitely complex system of working routines can a man eat his breakfast and then think about a new social order.

If we believe that—and I do—then it is up to us in the private sector to make our contributions to society so significant that there will be no vacuum for government to walk in and fill. The encroachments of government into private life have always been, to some degree, in response to default.

This means that we must take the initiative in seeking out places where we can make our greatest contributions. As long as we react defensively—in fact, as long as we merely react—we are not going to handle ourselves wisely. We will always be off balance, we will not be poised, and we will not act from strength.

We will be allowing others, who know less than we do of our capabilities and potentials, to choose the playing fields on which we should play.

This does not mean that business alone should dominate or dictate society's total answers or be defiant about those proposed by others, but it does mean that business should be affirmative, not passive.

And then comes the question, "How much?"

The real question for corporate management is not—never has been—whether it should be socially involved. The only question is, "How much?"

There are no pat answers, and never will be. But in principle, this question is no different from any other question of resource allocation. For that is what this boils down to—the old business of resource allocation in modern dress. It has long been my conviction that dealing with the question of "how much" is one of the highest of the management arts. How much earnings should be paid out and how much retained for future growth? How much for shareholders, how much for employees? How much for this product line and how much for that one?

Now the new question: how much for social performance? And believe me, in the words of the King of Siam, " 'tis a puzzlement."

A few efforts are being made to quantify the answer. Bank of America, for one, has engaged in some experimental efforts to set up a social cost budget, as well as the conventional economic cost budget, and has asked its accountants to place detailed cost estimates on what bank management considers its major social responsibilities.

Let me offer an oversimplified example of some of the factors that can be incorporated into a social cost budget. Suppose that a plant manager decides not to install pollution-control devices on his factory smokestacks. He has saved the cost of buying and installing the controls. But how much will the added pollution cost him in the long run? Polluted air makes the neighborhood around the factory a less desirable place to live, potential workers move away and housing will begin to deteriorate. To get trained workers, the factory manager finds he must pay higher wages: first, because employees have to travel extra miles to get to work, and second, because the factory is now situated in a less desirable area. The manager may find that his secretary is afraid to work after five o'clock, and he may end up paying her taxi fare home. Unemployed residents of the neighborhood resent the fact that the factory hires its workers from outside the neighborhood. The factory manager has to hire extra guards and beef up his security precautions. Eventually the factory may have to relocate to a better neighborhood.

I have exaggerated the situation for the purpose of illustration. But the question is a valid one. If a company ignores its social responsibility—installing pollution controls, for example—does it really save money? Is the money it saves in the short run worth the cost of higher wages, extra security measures, and possible relocation? In my example, the answer is obviously "no" to both questions. But the answer is not always so obvious. And the question is by no means as limited to one's own plant as in this example, because there often are social costs of a broader kind: if smoke and fumes compel householders to paint their houses twice as often, that is a social cost; if the same fumes create a health problem, the resultant health care constitutes a social cost. These pose an economic and an ethical question: who should pay these costs?

But I suspect that in this, as in other applications of this management art, the real test is going to be in the marketplace. The market—in this case the stock market—can sort out investment decisions. If management believes the investor will reap a greater total reward from a program that postpones some immediate return for the sake of later earnings, any investor who doesn't like that program—who doesn't want to wait—can always sell his stock. Of course, if enough of the stockholders think management is not making sense with its "plow back and wait," they can always throw management out and get a new one.

I could have said that the answer to the question of how much is "try it and see"—and that would not have been entirely facetious. Because, even with the best of measuring devices, analytical tools and quantitative guidelines, the art of judgment is still required.

If you spend too much, your shareholders may throw you out. If you spend too little, the voters may throw you out. If you are good enough, you will find that invisible line, the point of balance between the two. That is why it is called "the *art* of management."

I feel strongly that we must keep the principle of volunteerism alive in America—and we will not do it if we turn to government, or default to government, every time there is a problem to be solved. The corporation is, of course, not the only vehicle through which people can channel their voluntary efforts, but it is one of the greatest mechanisms ever devised for the mobilizing and focusing of resources—physical as well as human resources.

Fortunately, there is no present indication that the game is going by default.

In spite of all the confusing debate, in spite of the difficulty of trying to quantify what is right, the enlightened leaders of business have not chosen to sit on the sidelines or to adopt any "wait and see" stance. Individual companies in considerable number have continued and have expanded their social programs; and major associations and federations of business have aligned themselves on the side of corporate social responsibility.

The Committee for Economic Development (CED) is a business-supported organization composed of two hundred leading businessmen and educators and devoted to developing, through research and discussion, findings and recommendations that may be guides to public and business policy. CED, in 1971, published a seventy-four-page report summarizing a five-year study of social problems that might be ameliorated by the efforts of business, especially large, professionally managed corporations. Entitled *The Social Responsibilities of Business Corporations*, the report in this paragraph summarized the attitude of its findings:

> Today it is clear that the terms of the contract between society and business are, in fact, changing in substantial and important ways. Business is being asked to assume broader responsibilities to society than ever before and to serve a wider range of human values. Business enterprises, in effect, are being asked to contribute more to the quality of American life than just supplying quantities of goods and services. Inasmuch as business exists to save society, its future will depend on the quality of management's response to the changing expectations of the public.

A recent addition to the literature on corporate social responsibility is *The Corporation in Transition*, a fifty-four-page booklet published by the Chamber of Commerce of the United States. A product of the Chamber's Council on Trends and Perspectives, this booklet does not necessarily represent official Chamber policy but is designed to alert Chamber members to emerging social and economic trends. The Chamber booklet concludes that "many business social goals are capable of being set, evaluated, and monitored in the same way as are traditional business goals," and it urges "involved" companies to develop a social auditing procedure.

Three statements in the booklet might seem surprising, coming from a Chamber of Commerce unit even without official endorsement; but they are evidence of the direction in which the thinking of corporate leaders is moving:

> Unless sizeable business firms initiate "social responsibility" policies now, government will force such action later.
>
> Adam Smith's "invisible hand" of perfect competition no longer is viewed as providing in all circumstances a match between individual self-interest and the general interest.
>
> The big corporation is in trouble today and, unless many of its basic production, marketing, employment and management policies change drastically, will continue to be in trouble in the 1970s and 1980s.

Being a corporate good citizen is not a new idea or a new role. The vast majority of companies and their executives have thought of themselves as corporate good citizens for decades. But the concept of what it means to be a "good citizen" has changed so drastically within one lifetime as to make it a completely new ball game.

It was much easier in an earlier day when life was simpler. In the early part of this century when Community Chests and their agencies were being formed, the problems were very visible and tangible. It is easy to understand a crippled child when you see his picture on the campaign poster with his crutches and braces. But the problems that grow out of the overcrowding of the cities and out of the speeding up of the pace of change are harder to grasp.

I would not want to suggest that everyone in business is addressing himself vigorously to the resolution of these social issues. The very nature of these current issues is such that not everyone quickly and easily understands their significance.

Business people are not usually selected or trained for dealing in abstractions and intellectual concepts. A few of what are called conceptualizers do emerge, and they play a vital role in any company that wants to move onto newer and higher ground. But such people are rare, and that is probably just as well; if everyone in the company were a conceptualizer, it would never get any work done. Corporations need what Anthony Jay has described as "the Yogis and the Commissars"—the thinkers and the doers. When they find the people who combine those two qualities, then they have the best of good things; and those are the people who usually find their way to the top of the corporate pyramid. They become the leaders whom others are willing to follow.

When these leaders lift their eyes off their own desks, when they turn their gaze outside their own company or their own industry to look at the broader problems of the world, they naturally tend to think first about problems in the economic realm. Not only do they feel the pressure of those problems, but their own experience and training prepare them to recognize and understand those problems. On the problems of the community and of society, they have tended to follow the lead of others whom they respect.

But now an increasing number of these leaders are coming to recognize that the community is *their* community; that the society is *their* society; and that they cannot divorce themselves, their families, or their companies from direct concern for the well-being of the community in which they live; nor can they divorce that community from the well-being of the total society.

One day in Washington, D.C., I was having luncheon with a group of faculty, administrators, and a few graduate students at one of the large universities. It was long before

I had become involved in any contact with student groups, and I had only recently become a college trustee. It was also long before any of the current wave of talking and writing about corporate social responsibility; so I was not prepared with an answer when one of the faculty members, a professor of economics, asked me why a businessman would spend his time working on some of the community and social activities I was described as being involved in.

After a bit of groping, I replied that there were two or three reasons. For one, I did not want to live or raise my children (by now, grandchildren) in a community that was socially or physically unhealthy. Poverty and untreated illness are not a good physical setting, let alone a good moral atmosphere, in which to live and raise children. Beyond that, the kind of recreational, and what we then called character-building, activities—Boy Scouts, Girl Scouts, Camp Fire Girls, boys' and girls' clubs—could not be best provided in a vacuum, for just a privileged few, even if we wanted to, and I didn't. Not only could the physical facilities and the supervision be better provided on a community-wide basis, but the purposes for which we would be doing it dictated that it be done that way. If we believed in the principles of tolerance and of equality of opportunity, and if we wanted our children to grow up believing in them, then we would have to practice them as we set up facilities for all children.

My examples focused on children, as I told the professor, because they were the easiest to visualize. But the same principle, of creating the kind of community in which you would want to live yourself, applied throughout all the things that one might do to help others through community and social activity.

If we want to reduce it to the most crass self-interest, I said to the professor, a businessman could justify every minute he would spend on such activities, in purely economic terms. There is no market, above a subsistence level, among nonproductive people. Today our welfare policies and programs assure a minimum purchasing power for food, clothing and shelter, but the ability to buy the discretionary items that keep the economy flourishing depends on being adequately employed. That in turn depends on raising the whole level of competence of great groups of people who today cannot compete in the employment markets.

So if those who have the sophistication to know all that is involved in developing today's marketable skills—if those people want to sell their goods—they should pitch in and help to raise the earning power of a group who can represent a tremendous potential market.

And then, I told the professor, the third reason for doing all these things is simply that it's the right thing to do.

It would not be realistic to expect everyone in business to understand all the abstractions and subtleties involved in today's social problems. Not everyone in the thirteen colonies could expound on the principles embodied in the Declaration of Independence, the Constitution, or the Bill of Rights, either; but because respected leaders propounded and articulated them, they gained acceptance as the central issues to be debated and hammered out. That process is taking place now in our business establishment, with a few of the most enlightened and articulate leaders setting the pace and helping to formulate the rationale.

It is a healthy, wholesome symptom that this rationale is not slipping into the clichés and platitudes that would characterize a new ideology. It is being debated and tested as it goes along. Typical of the sorting and sifting process have been the inputs of men like Thomas J. Watson, Jr., until recently the board chairman of IBM. While completely subscribing to the doctrine that the business corporation must concern itself and involve itself in the problems of society, and must expect to pay its fair share of the cost of solving those problems, Mr. Watson raises a protesting hand against the idea that the costs of correcting generations-old problems—pollution problems, for example—should necessarily be borne entirely by the business firms that currently are carrying on the questioned practice. This entire area of cost allocation for social-improvement programs can be sticky, but it has already been shown, in a few cases where it has been tried, that people of good will looking at a problem in good faith can find formulas by which to measure who is responsible for what. Blind refusal to acknowledge that a problem exists, on the one hand, or vindictive attacks on those involved, on the other hand, are a poor foundation for solution of problems.

The former chairman of Xerox Corporation, Sol Linowitz, now chairman of the National Urban Coalition, has summed up eloquently the case for corporate involvement in society's problems. In his Koshland Lectures at the University of California he said:

To realize its full promise in the world of tomorrow, American business and industry—or at least the vast portion of it—will have to make social goals as central to its decisions as economic goals; and leadership in our corporations will increasingly have to recognize this responsibility and accept it.

Now more than ever before our corporations need not partial people or splinter specialists but leaders of breadth and vision to deal with the problems which confront us today and will be upon us tomorrow.

For the future corporate leader will need a world view far more expansive than has ever been required in the past. He will have to be a person who can communicate with other people in other places . . . who will recognize that things human and humane are even more important than the computer, the test tube, or the slide rule . . . who will try to see our problems as part of total human experience . . . and who will be able to understand something of what yesterday teaches us about today.

I believe it is the responsibility of business to seek out such men and women and develop them for the good of the corporation and for the benefit of society at large.

In an interview preceding the lectures, Mr. Linowitz stressed the imperative of "business' perception that its own future and its own interests are inextricably entwined with the future and interests of society."

For my own part, I am convinced there will be sweeping changes in the corporation over the next decade as business adapts itself to a changing external environment. Here are a few of the changes that I foresee:

1. Despite the Friedman argument to the contrary, business will become more socially oriented, more aware that its long-term survival demands such social orientation.

2. The profit maximization yardstick as the final arbiter of company performance will not meet the needs of the years ahead and will be increasingly replaced by a broader concept of long-term profit optimization—a process already underway in many companies. This concept will put far more weight on the total environment in which business operates than we have ever done in the past. There is now and will continue to be a growing realization among businessmen that nobody can expect to make profits—or to have any meaningful use for profits—if the whole fabric of the society is being ripped to shreds.

3. The investment community will recognize, as never before, that business involvement in societal needs is a sine qua non for long-term investment performance. Already some security analysts and some institutional fund managers are trying to factor a company's social performance into their investment analysis and decision.

4. The organization chart of most businesses will flatten out. Technologically savvy, innovative and highly motivated young people will not be content with the apprenticeship system of management development and progression that has characterized most large companies. They will demand more interface with top management and less bureaucracy, hierarchy, and red tape. And they will get it because we can stand a good deal of pruning around and about the bureaucratic structure.

5. There will be a change in value structure in the internal milieu of the corporation. Encouraged by activist youth, spurred on by their own observation, and dissatisfied in middle years by the end product of their life-style, senior and middle-level management will begin to modify their own value system. Not only will this modified value system produce a more societally oriented executive corps, it will also spell an end to the era of the one-track mind, sixteen-hour-a-day executive whose sole preoccupation in life is his business. And this will be good for business in the classical sense of profits. For too long the businesses of this nation have been victimized by the bad decisions of the large corporation's version of Babbitt—the hard-driving corporate commissar whose life-style has made him too narrow to have vision, too officious to be humane, too rigid to hear, and too tired to be wise.

In short, over the next decade or so I see the business system of America evolving into more socially oriented, humane, and responsive institutions—and in the final analysis, more beneficial institutions—more beneficial to the society, to the employee, and to the shareowner. Businessmen are fond of quoting Alfred North Whitehead's famous dictum to the effect that "A great society is one in which businessmen think greatly about their function." Too often, I fear, the venerable philosopher-mathematician turned uneasily in his grave when his words were cited, for too often they were, and still are, used as a proof of legitimacy or as a comforting opiate. Whitehead was neither attempting to underline the legitimacy of business nor was he, I suspect, interested in providing the businessman with an opiate. Rather, he was saying that the businessman must think in broader terms; must fit the needs and aspirations of his time and his society into his business planning. In this sense, Whitehead's dictum becomes a provocative warning and accurate guidepost for business management in the tumultuous decade of change which lies ahead of us.

YOUR OWN CUBIC FOOT
OF CLEAN AIR

10

Environment introduces a new factor into the social responsibility equation.

Someone has said: "There is no way that the private enterprise system or the market system can provide you with your own cubic foot of clean air." If ever we doubted the words of John Donne that "No man is an island," we find proof in the whole concept of the environment.

No longer can we assume that a project or a business venture will be publicly acceptable just because it will be profitable. Or just because it will "produce a highly marketable new product." Or just because it will "create jobs."

The public is saying that to destroy an irreplaceable resource to create jobs is like eating your seed corn—only worse. You might be able to borrow seed corn for a new start, the environmentalists say, but you can't borrow a river, a mountain, or a forest.

And the environmentalists have been gaining broad public support for the view that a "resource" is not just a mineral deposit or a source of energy. Included among the resources to be protected—the endangered resources—are ingredients that contribute only to beauty, and that word "only" would be challenged by the growing public view.

It is an assertion that the economic shall not be the only criterion in measuring the propriety of a development: the aesthetic shall be included in the test.

It is not a new concept. The admonition that "Man shall not live by bread alone" has come to us from the Book of Matthew. But it is a concept that got elbowed aside and run over in the scramble for economic growth. Even now, for all the gains that have been made, the support is by no means unanimous.

The resistance comes from a surprising variety of quarters. It would be expected that the companies or individuals promoting a development would resist any interference with it. And since jobs are to be involved, labor has generally not been allied with the environmentalists. But the resistance and suspicion have not stopped there: racial, minority, and related social issues have been injected into the contest. Not only have the racial minorities in America viewed the environmental thrust here as a threat to them, but their national counterparts—the so-called "developing countries" of the world—have taken a similar stance in international movements. At the United Nations Conference on the Human Environment, held in Stockholm in June 1972, these less-developed countries were hostile to most of the proposals advanced to protect the endangered resources of the world. Whereas the delegates from the major nations showed plainly that they had come to Stockholm to join in seeking ways to develop positive environmental programs, the representatives of the less-developed countries seemed to have come there on the defensive, as if the Conference had been assembled to plot against their welfare.

Not all the resistance comes from these lower segments of the economic scale. Large groups in organized labor, including some of the more skilled crafts, have been aligned on the "jobs come first" front. It is understandable that all these resisting groups should be concerned, because much of what is being discussed is new and strange territory for them. When the new concepts run counter to lifelong beliefs and convictions, that is unsettling enough; when they represent an actual threat to a man's future and security, as in the case of some environmental issues, he is understandably shaken and likely to be defensive.

It is time to remind ourselves again, as I remarked earlier, that it is no solution to a problem to have apoplexy in the face of it. It is a time to back off calmly and take a look at how we got to the point where ecology is such an issue. That could be applied equally to other sensitive public issues. We should not be quick to judge or to condemn a point of view until we have looked at it through the opposition's eyes. Viewed in that way, the solutions may not always be "either/or" decisions; they may not have to involve victory for one and defeat for the other, but a new path devised by joint effort. Because the real goals in these environmental and social issues are common goals, not competitive or exclusive ones.

Thoughtful people in the business community are recognizing all this and are adjusting their corporate thinking to it. I know that the cynics will say, "Oh, yeah? I don't believe it." Let me cite one small example of what is happening: The Conference Board, formerly called the National Industrial Conference Board, is a national organization set up to guide and assist business by research and conference discussion of vital problems of management policy. Recently in New York City the Conference Board held one of its major national conferences on "The Environment and Public Policy." The announcement of the Conference opened with these words: "Today there are few who would dispute the need to ensure that environmental impact is given full consideration in the conduct of public or private enterprise." Ten years ago, or even five, I doubt that such a conference would even have been held, let alone be keynoted by such a statement.

Now, I had no illusions that the conference would see anything like unanimity on anything except that the issue was important enough to talk about. But that is a beginning. One of my Stanford professors used to cite the case of the missionary, early in this century, who returned from his work among the cannibal tribes in the South Pacific and was reporting on his work and his progress to the members of his church. When he concluded, one of the old parishioners spoke up and asked, "Have you actually cured the cannibals of their hideous practice of eating human flesh?" He replied, "No, but we've taught them to sit at a table and use a knife and fork."

While it was small comfort to the people who went into the pot, still it is a fact that when hostile people can be persuaded to sit down around a table together and discuss a problem it is the indispensable first step. They may be inclined at first to want to eat each other up, but there can never be mutual understanding without that step.

Meanwhile, the Great Uncommitted Middle—the people who are not directly involved in the confrontations but whose weight, shifted one way or the other, ultimately gives the determining shove to the force of public opinion —are having their say.

The dedication to growth—for example, the assumption that "Bigger Is Better"—is being challenged, and so effectively that the challenge cannot be ignored. What started as apparently facetious tongue-in-cheek movements, like Lesser Seattle and Lesser Los Angeles, are now bearing fruit in official government actions. In one area after another, cities and counties are adopting official policies that they do not want to grow—that their populations are to be leveled off at some fixed figure, and that no utilities will be provided to serve anything larger. In the 1972 election in California, the voters took a look at a century-old pattern of steady population increase and turned their backs on it. The issue nominally did not involve population: it was an initiative measure to apply tight controls over any further development along California's coastline. But when warned by the opposition to the measure that if they locked up the seacoast against development, and therefore against generation of nuclear power, there might be a critical shortage of power a few years hence, the proponents didn't just say, "Then burn coal" or "Burn oil." No, they said, for the first time, "Maybe we don't need to use all the power we are now using and propose to use. Maybe we should stop and take a look at *why* we seem to need so much new power." And the majority of the voters—a substantial majority—joined in support of this position.

This was heresy—but it happened. And its happening cannot be ignored.

We have seen that there is a rising sentiment against growth per se. The agitation for Zero Population Growth is one expression of that feeling. More than three years ago I started warning my associates and friends that they should not laugh off Zero Population Growth, that it is a growing movement and one that we must consider in our plans. Is there any part of our economy that isn't dedicated to the Great God Growth? Has anyone calculated what would happen if growth suddenly stopped? I don't *yet* know of any such calculation that has been done, any economic model that has been constructed on a ZPG basis. We'd better do some calculating because it just *could* happen. I will only repeat what I said in my earlier warnings: that, as profoundly disturbing and unsettling as such a flattening-out would be, it wouldn't necessarily be fatal. It would compel us to shift from a preoccupation with quantity to more concern for quality.

It is one more evidence of the changing values and evidence that people are challenging and reexamining—not always rejecting, but testing and reexamining—assumptions they had lived with all their lives.

Where the environmental problem involves an industrial

activity that has gone on for a long period without public protest, such as production of smog-producing automobiles (possibly even with public encouragement, as in the case of stream-polluting or air-polluting industries that had been solicited to come into the community), it has been suggested that the cost of making changes to meet the new environmental requirements should be paid or shared by government, and that companies put out of business by ecological regulations should be indemnified.

These are proper issues to debate. Where there are social benefits, social costs might be recognized. But all through our history, businesses have persisted or suffered because of new public patterns. Some have been outlawed, such as the making and selling of some patent medicines, fireworks, and the like. Others have become obsolete, like buggy whips, button hooks, and flypaper. Still others have been by-passed, like the roadside restaurant or hotel stranded by the relocation of a highway. The downgrading of property values by rezoning is a comparable hazard.

Rarely has anyone been indemnified for being caught in such a tide of change. Is there a difference this time? If there is, it should be possible to establish it as a matter of equity.

Establishing criteria by which to judge whether a company or individual is entitled to such indemnity is not a simple undertaking. Legal and other authorities who have addressed themselves to the problem tend to agree that the ultimate solution will be to fall back on the ancient principles of equity; but the standards that guide the courts of equity—the standards of "fundamental fairness"—are not easy to apply to a field that has so many variables.

At one end of the spectrum, a speculator who has gambled on the hope of enhanced land values but is blocked from his subdivision plans by new environmental restraints may seem clearly to have no more equitable right to indemnity than any other speculator whose projected profits do not materialize. At the other end of the scale, an industry that had located in a remote area specifically zoned for its type of industry, had had all its waste and emissions systems approved by the appropriate authorities, and had operated for years before population pushing in around it brought new regulations requiring costly modifications—that industry may seem to have grounds for claiming that some part of its costs should be borne by the community.

Even on the two extreme cases I have cited there would, at this stage, be hot debate as to how they were to be treated. But in between these extremes, the gradations are as infinite as the shadings of the color spectrum—and not nearly so orderly, because a multitude of complicating and conflicting factors often enter into the environment picture.

To a limited extent, the pricing mechanism can help to balance social costs against social benefits, but only when there is universal demand for the product.

The propriety of some degree of public sharing in these social costs has been recognized in California by the enactment of a Pollution Control Financing Authority Act, under which the authorities may aid corporations in financing construction of certain types of pollution control facilities. Under this program, the corporation's costs will be lower because the equipment is paid for out of the proceeds of tax-exempt revenue bonds which carry a lower interest rate.

I would be both misleading and unfair if I gave the impression that all industries were sitting idly by, waiting for government action to compel them to clean up their pollution. Many, many companies have taken their own initiative and gone to great expense to correct conditions—many of which had gone on for decades without anyone even questioning them.

Some other companies have actually encouraged government intervention because they were in highly competitive industries and felt that if they undertook the expense alone and others did not follow suit, they would not be able to survive competitively.

One of the more heated—and predictable—controversies has been triggered by the publication in 1972 of a book entitled *The Limits to Growth*. Published under the sponsorship of the so-called Club of Rome, it is the first account of the findings of a study carried out by a team at MIT examining "the five basic factors that determine, and therefore ultimately limit, growth on this planet—population, agricultural production, natural resources, industrial production and pollution." It presents a computer simulation and mathematical model forecasting disastrous results if the present exponential growth in these basic factors continues even for a few decades.

The attacks on the book and on its conclusions have mainly been focused on the mathematical treatment of factors that contain so many social and other variables. One critic dismissed the entire conclusion as "pretentious nonsense": without defending the mathematics or any of the exact timetables of the projections, I am compelled to say that the concerns expressed in the book cannot be dismissed so lightly. Pretentious the model may be, but nonsense it is not. What real difference does it make whether we run out of space and out of resources in forty years or four hundred? The principle is the same. In any case, it is clear that exponential growth applied to finite resources can have only one ultimate result: trouble. Debating over when or where the trouble will hit is idle.

Some of those who criticize the findings of the MIT team and who view all such writers as "false prophets of doom" base their complacency about the environment on their confidence that human ingenuity will find answers to all the shortages that might result as we deplete our nonrenewable resources. Their attitude is uncomfortably reminiscent of Dickens' Mr. Micawber who always was sure that "something will turn up."

If no other conclusion of the *Limits* book were accepted,

one alone would make it worth heeding: that "man is forced to take account of the limited dimensions of his planet and the ceilings to his presence and activity on it."

It is possible that so much focus on mere survival has led us to overlook a higher order of issues. As Barkley and Seckler said in *Economic Growth and Environmental Decay*, "Those who prophesy extinction are not sufficiently serious about the environment. The problems that must be overcome for survival are comparatively trivial, for survival can be achieved through manipulation of the physical world. But the environment is a social as well as a physical phenomena. Indeed, alterations in the entire range of man's physical, biological, institutional and social fabric may be required before serious problems of the quality of life can be solved."

The sharpened awareness of what has happened to our environment does indeed bring into focus the whole question of quality of life.

Throughout most of my life, "standard of living" has been the term used to measure whether people were living well or badly, and to measure relatively how well or badly one group of people were living as compared with another. Standard of living, in turn, was measured entirely in physical units, if not indeed monetary units, so that there was virtually no difference between standard of living and per capita income.

I have long felt that there was need for a new formula, and I have one that is useful at least for each individual to apply in making his own choices as to where and how he is to live. By this formula, standard of living would be stated as: the number of hours per week that one is able to spend doing the things that give him satisfaction. If one likes to live in the country but the urban area is so congested or transportation is so poor, or the freeways so crowded that it takes him two hours each way to get to and from the country, his standard of living is thereby reduced.

If he likes to play golf or tennis but the smog is so bad

as to make outdoor exertion unpleasant or unsafe, his standard of living is thereby reduced.

If he gets satisfaction from hearing and observing birds but lack of trees in an overcrowded city has driven birds beyond his reach, his standard of living suffers.

Whatever his interests, whatever gives him satisfactions, if he is not able to engage in them, it does not matter what keeps him from being "able"—lack of sufficient income, lack of hours because of commuting time, or lack of resources because civilization has driven them out—he still has a lowered standard of living no matter what his bank statement may show.

There are those who will not equate birds and flowers and trees with a standard of living; those who have always scoffed at such books as Rachel Carson's classic, *Silent Spring*. After the oil-spill crisis at Santa Barbara, when there was great outcry from nature lovers and conservationists over the destruction of shore birds, one state official sneeringly dismissed all those concerned as "the bird-and-bunny people."

It appalls me to think how empty life would be on this planet if Rachel Carson's warnings were not heeded and her predictions were to come true. Elsewhere in this book I have referred to the deep-seated psychological need that exists for people to have some beauty in their lives. Without even basing the case on such scientific evidence, I am willing to content myself with the testimony of the poet Sadi who wrote:

If of thy mortal goods thou art bereft,
And from thy slender store two loaves alone to thee are
    left,
Sell one, and with the dole
Buy hyacinths to feed thy soul.

OWNERSHIP OR
STEWARDSHIP?

11

A new concept of private property has emerged from the confrontations on the environment.

Ours has been and in many ways still is a frontier civilization, a frontier life. Throughout our entire national history we have been exploring and taking possession of a new country. One consequence of this "pioneer syndrome" has been that whenever things got too sticky where they were the pioneers would push on to a new place—a place where there was still plenty of room. The frontiersman solved many of his human problems by running away from them.

But there was another consequence, a corollary to this first one. It was the illusion that space and resources were inexhaustible. Combining that point of view with one of the prime motivations of the pioneer as he moved West— the urge to own a piece of land of his own—breeds an attitude toward private property that seems as basic and as sacred as the Bill of Rights. Now, all of a sudden it becomes a focal point in the whole ecology battle.

It has seemed to be an axiom of American life that a man's property was his to use as he saw fit. That had been tacitly assumed to be part of what was meant when he spoke of "the right of private ownership of property," one of his sacred rights in a democracy. "A man's home is his castle" we would say, without stopping to think whether that covered the whole issue of what goes on inside that castle.

But that never has been an unlimited, unqualified right. The limitations applied from time to time have been those that were important to the life of that day. From the beginning, the right of privacy, of freedom from trespass, freedom from unwarranted search and the like has been protected. But the use of property to disturb the peace, to create a public nuisance, to endanger health or safety has long been subject to limitation.

Now there is added to that limitation the doctrine that ownership of private property does not bestow unlimited right to alter the character of that property. Heretofore, the limitations have recognized that neighbors and other contemporaries have a right to be protected from improper use of property. The new doctrine adds future generations as having the right to enjoy the property unchanged in character unless the changes have been publicly declared to be in the public interest.

What this doctrine introduces is the element of stewardship. It says, in effect, "This property is yours to use, and for your children and their children to use, unless you choose to sell it to someone else, which you have the right to do. But each of you who comes into possession of it has an obligation to pass it on in as good condition as when you received it. No one of you has the unlimited right, during his brief tenure of holding the property, to make irreversible changes in its character without public consent." While we should be free to enjoy and to make any use of the land that does not injure others, we are at all times stewards of that land, responsible to our contemporaries and to posterity for proper and judicious treatment of the land while it is in our care.

So, while it could be "every man for himself" when space

and resources seemed unlimited, it becomes the difference between a society and a jungle when the consequences of "every man" have an impact on everyone else. So it is "Every man for himself as long as he takes nothing away from anyone else." There is nothing new about that principle, but it comes as a shock to many when it is applied to the use of property.

It will come as even more of a shock if people in Alabama or Wyoming or some equally remote spot begin telling you, in Illinois or Texas, that you cannot mine or log or dam streams in the way you used to. But don't be surprised to see it happen.

We have grown up assuming that what New Mexicans did to New Mexico was the New Mexicans' business, and what the Montanans did to Montana was their buisness, and so on across the country. But there is a growing philosophy that says, "Go ahead and do whatever you want to do with your own little span of life, but when you get all through, leave the country the way you found it."

Today's laws may not support it, but the same doctrine of stewardship that asserts rights for posterity as well as contemporaries carries with it the principle that any citizen of this country—if not, indeed, of the world—has a stake in what happens to land anywhere. States' rights and state sovereignty, which already have lost much of their traditional force, are likely to lose another round on this issue. Laws have a way of being amended to keep pace with the will of the majority, and any laws that stand in the way of the stewardship principle are likely to be reshaped.

The issue gets sharply drawn in cases like that of the strip-mining controversy that is raging in many parts of the country. While the mining projects themselves are largely in the mountain states, where coal deposits are located, the protests are coming from every section of America. The "energy crisis," which is providing the rationale for all manner of programs sponsored by electric power companies, gas companies, oil companies, coal companies—nuclear power plants, pipelines, oil import quotas, oil shale research and the like—has also been used as the *raison d'être* for the wave of strip-mining for coal.

Today, virtually every major oil and coal company in America has moved into Montana and the neighboring coal states to buy or lease coal deposits. Whether the deposit is a long-standing holding or only newly acquired, the assumption had been the same: that the owner has the right to mine it as he chooses. But new regulations in many of the states are limiting that right.

As a minimum, most of the states are now requiring that any topsoil or "over-burden" removed in strip, dredge, or other types of surface mining be restored and in the same relative order. Some of the mining companies claim that they leave the area more attractive and more usable than they found it because they have created lakes for fishing, boating, and other recreational uses where only a bleak, flat prairie existed before. When corporations do this kind of thing and do it well, they do have an arguable point. But their claim is challenged by conservation groups on the ground that many of the stripped areas, far from being "bleak" or "ugly," were in fact unique parts of a fast-disappearing wilderness.

On the same ground, conservationists are fighting to save the few remaining marshes and estuaries around our larger cities. For most of our history, the filling in of these marshes had been called "reclamation"—the reclaiming of "waste" lands. Only as the marshes disappeared did it become evident that many rare species of bird life (as well as plant and underwater life) were disappearing with them; and as this piece of the beauty and charm of the area departed, some of the quality of life departed with it.

In all these cases, the issues, the trade-offs, and the priorities are debatable. At least now they *are* being debated, and a case is having to be made, before an irreplaceable resource is destroyed, that the immediate necessity is so great as to outweigh all other responsibilities.

The doctrine of stewardship has another implication that has been too little recognized. It applies also to the rights and the obligations of colleges and their students.

During the height of the campus unrest, there were riots and other incidents in which students "trashed," burned, bombed, and destroyed college properties in the name of enforcing their "rights" to "demand" what they called "relevant education." To destroy a laboratory, let alone an irreplaceable library, under any kind of pretext is such a hideous, wanton piece of vandalism and savagery that it hardly deserves patient discussion. But because a wave of violence could again be generated, and because calmer students might need the support of a rationale to counter the inflammatory rhetoric, I would offer this:

—Changes that are made in response to today's pressures should not be allowed to destroy values that will be important to future generations.

—The college today is the sum-total of knowledge, libraries, facilities and resources contributed by generations of those who have helped to build it.

—Trustees are more than a name: they hold the college in trust—not to freeze it or keep it unchanged, but to assure that future generations receive it as a vital, growing force.

—Students in exercising their proper right of criticism, of dissent and protest should keep perspective.

They are not the first generation, nor will they be the last, to use what the college has to offer.

The college was neither created *by* them nor created exclusively *for* them.

PROGRESS OR GREED?

12

While greed is at the root of many environmental and other problems of society, greed is not the exclusive shortcoming of any one class or group. Nor is it a twentieth-century phenomenon. The real estate developer who squeezed houses onto every inch of his land without regard to the effect on the natural terrain, or without regard to the surrounding community, had his counterpart example in the good people of Philadelphia a hundred years or more before. Their greed for real estate profits led them to crowd commercial buildings so close to Independence Hall that visitors wanting to see the birthplace of our nation could hardly find it. It remained for more public-spirited people of this century to initiate the movement to restore the site to something more nearly resembling its original condition, or at least to a condition more fitting to a national landmark.

When a large corporation proposes to come into a new area with an industrial plant that may generate harmful or disagreeable by-products—air-polluting fumes, water-polluting wastes, land-scarring excavation or whatever—it may be opposed by elements in the community who fear the dam-

aging effects of those by-products. But it also will usually
be strongly supported by other elements in the same community: some will be landowners, who expect to sell at a
profit direct to the new company; others will be owners of
nearby land, who expect their property to increase in value
because of the homes and shops that will have to be built
to serve the new development; some will be present store
owners, like the "Pop and Mom" corner grocers, who expect increased business from the new residents (and who
are most often disillusioned because the new growth at-
tracts new competition in the form of larger chain stores
from outside); and some will be real estate brokers who
expect generally accelerated turnover in the area.

Not that any of these local supporters will usually acknowledge the reasons why they favor the new industry.
Their public endorsements will usually be based on the
"need for payrolls to balance our seasonal economy" or
"the need for a broadened tax base to relieve the burden on
homeowners." (Again disillusionment is in the offing; actual
experience has shown almost without exception that when
a formerly rural or residential area has gone industrial, the
property tax rates have risen. The new labor force drawn
into the area has required public services of a kind and in a
volume out of proportion to their contribution to the tax
rolls.)

The virgin forest that is denuded by the giant lumber
company is no more denuded than the area that is logged by
the small, independent "gyppo" logging operators who de-
scend upon a forested area on a "clean-up-and-get-out" basis.
(Note: "clean up" does not refer to the condition in which
they leave the forest!)

When I point my finger at greed, it is not simply to deplore it or to moralize about it. It deserves to be deplored
and it deserves to be moralized about, but this book is not
a moral tract. We can save the moralizing for another time

and place, and even then, because greed is so universal a potential, I fear that none of us has the right to cast the first stone.

My purpose in focusing on it here is to identify it; to help people—both the people who practice it and the people who are its victims—to recognize it for what it is. For our great human capacity for self-deception enables us often to conceal our own greed even from ourselves, and to mask it in such pious terms that we convince ourselves that we are acting only from the loftiest motives. If it is not a public-service motive, like "progress," or "jobs," or "balanced economy," then it at least is a matter of justice. The small landowner, whose family may have operated a dairy for three generations at the edge of town, will see subdivisions pushing out toward him as a consequence of the new industrial plant, and he will say, "We have hung onto this land, grubbing out a poor living while we waited for the town to grow out this way. Now we are entitled to our just reward." Which is all well and good, as long as it is recognized for what it is—a self-serving rationale—and is not allowed to influence others in the community to approve an undesirable development out of sympathy for the poor property owner.

The fact that nearly every religion and philosophy identifies greed as one of the cardinal sins is evidence that it is a universal tendency. It grows out of the most normal and natural of impulses—the instinct for security. This human instinct is a vice only when it becomes so exaggerated in its proportions that it distorts and dominates human behavior.

My wife describes it more succinctly: "Greed is the cancer cell that grows when the drive for security becomes malignant."

Greed, in the sense of hunger for money or its material equivalents, has its twin in overwhelming ambition for power or position. And those seeking that power are not all in business, large or small. Many of our government bureaus have been among our worst offenders. Again, what had started as a good, constructive force to serve a genuine need has frequently become a vested interest that has sought to perpetuate itself in power by generating political pressure for projects and appropriations.

The U.S. Army Engineers, now known as the Corps of Engineers, is one of the clearest examples.

Originally created to serve a strictly military purpose, the Corps' activities have reached deeper and deeper into the civilian life of communities not remotely related to the military. Because inland waterways and navigation were important to the military, flood control on navigable waters became a large and larger part of the Corps' concern; and flood control means dams and water storage, often accompanied by generation of hydroelectric power. So any local group anywhere in the country that has wanted to dam a river or a creek has thought of the Corps as a possible source of funds; and the Corps has done nothing to discourage this thinking.

With eleven division and thirty-seven district offices staffed by about two hundred military officers and more than thirty thousand civilian employees, this is a bureaucracy that can prosper only by having projects. Projects need Congressional appropriations, and appropriations need political support. While the Corps does not lobby, it has a powerful lobby behind it in the local pressure groups that may benefit by the project.

As in any bureaucracy, the prestige—and advancement—of each project manager and supervisory officer depend upon the projects over which he presides, so, far from sitting back and waiting for projects to come to them, these officers actively encourage the development of projects, and counsel with potential applicants on how to present and develop support for their proposals.

Now that an estimated 90 percent of the nation's water resources have already been "developed" in some manner, the hunger for projects to occupy this bureaucracy is so great as to lead them into programs that at best are marginal and at worst are horrendous scars on the landscape. One of the last of the great pictorial-editorial jobs by *Life* magazine before its demise was an exposé of the brutally ravaging effects of a typical Corps job in making a concrete ditch, with barren shores, of a formerly winding wooded stream.

The sense of stewardship was as completely lacking in such projects as in the worst examples of private real estate development; and while they were not done for private pecuniary gain, they involved the same principle of putting self-interest, of one or another kind, ahead of the public interest.

The highway-building fraternity, often referred to as the highway lobby, is the other of the two most conspicuous government entities that started from urgent necessity and has gone on to be an ominous environmental threat. While the Corps of Engineers and the highway fraternity share many characteristics in common—the need to have projects that will keep a large bureaucracy employed, the existence of a "civil-industrial complex" that rivals or outshines the "military-industrial complex"—the highway network is unique in the degree to which it has reached into every state, county, and city of America and built its power as almost a law unto itself.

Because there is such a pooling of self-interest in support of it—state and local governments wanting to share in it; road-machinery, building material, automobile and truck manufacturers and distributors; automobile associations, oil companies; and so on and on—the gasoline-tax fund has for more than a generation been a sacred cow. Any attempt to divert the funds to other than highway purposes—even to other transportation programs that might relieve congestion on the highways—has until very recently been successfully resisted. Even the name of the federal fund was changed a few years ago to the Highway Trust Fund, thus cloaking it with even more inviolability.

But it has not been the jealous guarding of the funds— irritating though that has been at times—that has aroused increasing resentment and even fear of the highway lobby. It has been its arrogant and often ruthless use of its power in ways that totally ignored all other values.

When highway engineers—for whatever reasons or by whatever calculations—decide that a new freeway should be built or an old highway relocated, they have the power of eminent domain to put it where they want it regardless of what it does to the area it passes through. It can destroy neighborhoods, destroy historic landmarks, destroy scenic values, create an asphalt, cement and steel blight, and in most jurisdictions there is no one to stop them. Theoretically the legislatures of the several states could control them, but until recently there has been little inclination to try to curb them because the bloc of political power supporting them has been too formidable.

The arrogance of power, however, invited its own downfall, and while the highway hierarchy is far from tumbling from its seat of power, signs are appearing to indicate that its days of living in untouchable immunity are numbered. The highway-aid bill signed into law by President Nixon in August of 1973 provides money for mass transit—the first time since the Highway Trust Fund was created that Congress has agreed to spend it for anything but highways.

When the proposal to create a Redwoods National Park in California was being debated in Congress, it provided a full-scale laboratory demonstration of how self-interest can be rationalized to sound public-spirited.

The purpose of the park project was to save from the logger's axe these oldest and largest of all living things—the last virgin stand of these giant redwoods remaining in private hands, and including some of the most beautiful and perfect specimens ever seen by modern man. Naturally the lumber companies owning the stands were reluctant to have them taken over by the government—even if adequately compensated—because it meant some curtailing of supplies for their mills.

But the principal argument that was made against the Park was that it would deprive people of jobs. Opponents of the project carefully calculated how many people would be employed in cutting down each of these majestic beauties, in hauling them to the sawmills, in shipping them out into the market, in using them to build houses—completely ignoring the fact that each of these jobs could be provided only once as the tree was destroyed, whereas the same tree could provide value forever as a living thing. Not only does it offer the spiritual values of peaceful beauty and the evidence of the continuity of a life that existed on earth before Christ was born, but in pure monetary terms it will probably give employment to infinitely more people all over the world as a tourist attraction than it would as a destroyed tree. But greed made many local citizens willing to sacrifice these ageless monarchs for the sake of their immediate gain.

The confluence of local "cashing-in" greed with the highway builder's bulldozing callousness brought tragicomic results to another part of California.

The Mother Lode area, in the foothills of the Sierra Nevada, is where gold was first discovered on this continent. It became the scene of the dramatic Gold Rush in 1849. A century later, this strip of gold country, because it was historically, scenically, and architecturally picturesque, became a tourist mecca. Thinking to cash in on its commercial tourist possibilities, some of the local business people promoted a new superhighway so that more people could come and visit the old ghost towns. But then what happened? In order to put the wide, modern highway through the middle of the towns, the highway people tore down some of the very buildings, the very landmarks, that the highway was bringing people to see!

(My wife says these bulldozer-happy engineers must think they have Biblical sanction from the Book of Isaiah, 40:4: ". . . and every mountain and hill shall be made low; and the crooked shall be made straight, and the rough places plain"!)

So the youth and others who swing their clubs solely at "big business" and "large corporations" as the social culprits may be missing some very important targets. "Little guys" and government agencies may contribute their share of private self-interest versus the public interest. The *real* target in any case should be not "who" but "what"—and "why."

Each new proposal that will use land, space, or other resources should be examined for its social benefits weighed against its social costs, regardless of who proposes it.

Slogans, clichés, and flag-waving should not be allowed to camouflage self-serving projects that damage the public interest. Nor should projects be automatically condemned because someone might benefit. Not only is it impossible to eliminate all personal benefit from public projects, but there is no reason to do so provided the rewards are in proportion to the contribution. Many publicly beneficial undertakings have been motivated by someone's hope of gain or of fame; the important thing is to examine each one to be sure that that hope is not the *only* motive, cloaked in high-sounding phrases.

Such evaluation is not easy, but it should be done, and under the full spotlight of public scrutiny. Too many undesirable programs have been allowed to slip through by pure default. Apathy and the fear of being thought "unpatriotic" or "lacking in civic pride" have silenced many a voice that should have spoken up.

THE QUALITY OF LIFE

13

As I was approaching my fiftieth birthday, I was lunching one day with a classmate of my college days. As we compared notes and brought each other up-to-date on what we had been doing (each of us trying to impress the other with how busy and important we were), my friend said he rarely had time to take a vacation.

I turned to him and asked, "Roy, has it ever occurred to you that, on the basis of three-score-and-ten, you and I may have only twenty more springtimes on this earth—only twenty more times to see wildflowers, to see fruit trees in bloom, to see the earth at its freshest? Each one of those you miss is a piece taken out of your life."

I felt doubly badly later, because he didn't live to see even one of those twenty springtimes.

I tell this tale as a reminder that quality of life is more than an environmental thing, more than a matter of protecting life against negative influences. It is a positive, affirmative thing. The quality of life must be deliberately sought after. If I may cite Maslow again, his studies showed that the need for beauty, at least in some individuals, was very deep, and that ugliness was actually sickening to them. His experiments showed that the effects of ugliness were dulling and stultifying, and that, in strictly biological terms, one needs beauty as one needs calcium in the diet—it helps one to be healthier.

I should warn business executives: if you allow yourself to question your corporate priorities in terms of quality of life, it may start you thinking about your own personal priorities—and that can be dangerous! It may recall childhood tales of King Midas and compel some self-examination. When we were children, we were brought up on the fables of King Midas and King Croesus and other legendary misers. We solemnly shook our heads and clucked our tongues at the folly of anyone who would put such a high value on money—so high in the case of King Midas that he would even sacrifice his child to his love of money. A miser, to our innocent minds, was just the most miserable of creatures (even the word "miser-able" is derived from that word, denoting an impoverished spirit).

We all learned that we should look down upon such misguided mortals. We knew that we should view them with pity, if not with contempt, because they had such a poor sense of values. We didn't know the word "values" then—that came much later. But we knew that Midas and Croesus and the miser "put too much store" by money; that they put a false and exaggerated importance on it.

And yet, what are we but misers if we sacrifice all other values to our striving for business success? There are other ways of sacrificing families to money than having them turned into cold lumps of gold like Midas' child. We may rationalize and say that we don't do it just for love of money, that we are building something, that we are rendering a great public service, and so on and on. And we may be, but the yardstick by which our success is measured is usually preceded by a dollar sign.

When my family goes on a pack trip into the High Sierra —a camping, fishing or hiking trip—the first thing we do at the end of our traveling day is to spot a good place to camp.

We need a place with enough flat space for beds, sheltered flat space for our campfire, cooking, and eating area, a good supply of drinking water within easy reach, plenty of firewood, pasture and water for our horses, if any, and no marshes to breed mosquitoes.

The next thing we do is pitch camp: set up our "kitchen," make our beds, put up tents, if we are using tents, gather wood and water.

Having done all that, we relax.

After all, we didn't come to the mountains to work; we came to enjoy the mountains: to fish, or take pictures, or paint pictures, or climb rocks, or just "be"—looking, smelling, listening, feeling.

Is there a parallel, a lesson here? I think so.

I am afraid too many of us have developed the habit of crowding all of that kind of living into one brief period we call a vacation—two weeks or three weeks or, if we are doing better, a month. Provided, that is, we take the vacation. Provided we haven't let ourselves be sucked into that whirlpool, that vicious circle of "indispensability" in which we keep putting off vacations because we "can't get away right now." So we go on working longer hours, longer weeks, getting a little further behind so that it is harder to get away on a vacation . . . ad infinitum.

Even if we take the vacation as we should, that should not be the only time in a year that we relax, the only time that we enjoy and savor and appreciate the world around us. We should learn to make "mini-vacations" every month, every week, and every day, by stopping long enough to be aware and to savor. Just as we don't go into the mountains only to work, so we don't come into the world only to work. We should find great satisfaction in our work, but we also should remember that one of the reasons we work is to be able to afford to enjoy other things. So work should be both an end and a means.

We cannot turn away from our own dollar goals and reflect for long on what is involved in quality of life, for ourselves and for others, without discovering that many things are needed: on the material side, there are large pockets of poverty and hunger in the midst of undreamed-of plenty, while on the spiritual side, great groups of both the affluent and of those in want are saying that life has no meaning for them. Most of the organized movements have been aimed at the material imbalance; too little has been directed toward the thing that most distinguishes man from an animal —the life of the spirit.

The inseparability of the two needs has been summed up in a charming little piece by Charles A. Lindbergh entitled "Lessons from the Primitive." After asking rhetorically what he has learned from his civilization during his seventy years of life, he replies that the answer is trite in its simplicity:

"I have learned," he says, "that the goal of man is man himself, and that he, his spirit, and his environment are one, transmuting through space and time."

I referred in an earlier chapter to the Calvin Coolidge dictum that "the business of America is business." Rather than just rejecting that and leaving nothing in its place, I have preferred to turn that around and say "the business of business is America." But the ultimate and correct version should be "the business of business *and* of America is man."

If we buy that, then one basic decision that we all must face is that quality of life—the conditions under which we live—is more important than any numbers that can be entered on a balance sheet or an earnings statement or in a bank book.

What is more, it is important to *us*, to each of us individually—not just to some one else.

Until very recently, the social and environmental issues were treated on a kind of "we and they" basis. "We" were busy minding our own affairs; "they," in the form of some do-gooders, were messing around and getting in people's hair about a lot of remote things like caribou in Alaska and seagulls getting covered with oil on the beach in Santa Barbara. Now we suddenly wake up to find that these issues aren't so remote after all.

For generations we have been mouthing the cliché, "You can't stand in the way of progress." Now there is a new generation that is saying, "The hell you can't." That generation—and an increasing number of its elders—are saying, "Prove to us that it really is progress." In a sense, that is the essence of everything that is stirring and boiling and seething: thoughtful people in increasing numbers are asking about one thing after another, "Is it really progress— progress for the human condition?"

They are saying, in effect, "I have only one life to live on this earth. Will it be a better life for me if the stream where I used to fish is polluted by industrial wastes? Will it be a better life for me if my ears are shocked and my windows rattled every few minutes by sonic booms? Will it be a better life for me if the beach where I used to swim is polluted by sewage? Will it be a better life for me if I have no clean air to breathe?" They will ask, "Is this really progress? If it is, I don't need it."

And we shouldn't have to wait for them to ask the question, because these should be our questions, too. This deterioration of the quality of life isn't something that just happens to other people; when it happens, it happens to us, too.

It happens to corporation executives, too, and to their families, and to their employees, and to their shareholders, and to their customers.

That is why debating over "corporate social responsibility" is such arrant nonsense. Environmental and other social problems should get at least as much corporate attention as production, sales, and finance. The quality of life in its total meaning is, in the final reckoning, the only justification for any corporate activity.

Happily, there are corporations whose top officers have not lost their perspective, and whose sense of social responsibility tells them that neither the company nor its products are the final corporate goal. They see that the quality of life, the conditions under which people live, and the things that give meaning to their lives are the ultimate concern of all organized activity, corporate or otherwise.

THE ARROGANCE OF POWER

14

What does the bombing of Cambodia have to do with bulldozers pushing a freeway through a virgin stand of redwoods? What did American intervention in the 1965 revolution in the Dominican Republic have in common with a mining company desecrating a fertile valley with strip-mining and stream pollution?

The common ingredient is the arrogance of power.

An early advertisement for a popular mouthwash used to feature the line, "The insidious thing about halitosis is that you don't know you have it." The same lament can be made for the arrogance of power: its possessor rarely knows he (or it) has it. It's doubly insidious because it is so often cloaked in self-righteousness.

I have been dealing thus far in this book largely with domestic issues and relationships. If, however, we want to have good insight into our individual and national goals we should look at ourselves in the perspective of our posture in world affairs. When we do, we find that a large share of our worst problems, both at home and abroad, we have brought on ourselves because, with the best of intentions, we have acted with the arrogance of power.

Senator J. William Fulbright, Chairman of the Senate

Foreign Relations Committee, has been a controversial figure, but I am convinced that history will record him as a
wise and dedicated American who lives up to his own defi-
nition of a patriot: to be self-critical rather than self-
righteous. From the vantage point of his long and intimate
contact with world affairs, he has written:

> Power tends to confuse itself with virtue and a great
> nation is peculiarly susceptible to the idea that its power is
> a sign of God's power, conferring upon it a special responsi-
> bility for other nations—to make them richer and happier
> and wiser, to remake them that is, in its own shining image.
> Power confuses itself with virtue and also tends to take it-
> self for omnipotence.

We were twice able to save the Western world from
military defeat because we had built such a strong economy,
such a powerful productive machine—not because our political, economic, or social philosophies were necessarily the
right answers to be imposed upon the rest of the world. We
misinterpreted our own performance, and when the threat-
ened peoples of Europe hailed us as saviours, we took the
role too literally. Starting with the highly idealistic crusade
of Woodrow Wilson, we developed a national sense of
mission—a Saviour complex—that we have never lost.

It was not the first time that we felt and acted as if we
had been given divine appointment to impose God's will
on "less-civilized nations"—both Presidents McKinley and
Theodore Roosevelt so stated; but theirs were relatively
parochial undertakings in relation to Latin America and
other former Spanish territories. It remained for Wilson to
have a global sense of mission—"to save the world for
democracy"—not reckoning with the question whether
everyone in the world was ready for or receptive to democracy.

We were like the three Boy Scouts who reported to their
scoutmaster that as their good deed for the day they had

helped an old lady to cross the street.

"That's fine," said the Scoutmaster, "but why did it take three of you?"

"Well," they explained, "she didn't want to go."

Our new sense of power after World War II, when we were the only major industrial nation left intact in the entire world and had resources enough to help rehabilitate the economies of the "Free World," generated a spirit of arrogance that has distorted our sense of national purpose. I am satisfied that the Marshall Plan and the related aid programs were initiated with the most genuinely altruistic motives—that the power sense was an unfortunate by-product. But that sense—belief that because we were so strong and so prosperous we must have all the answers, and because other nations needed our economic help we had the right to impose those answers on them—has guided our foreign policy since World War II.

And it is one of the interesting, ironic facts of life that gratitude is a very strange emotion: gratitude often begets resentment. People who are helped and at first are grateful begin to resent the helper because he is a reminder of their own inadequacy. People elsewhere undoubtedly resented our opulence and our affluence and our power.

So when we went beyond helping and began to throw our weight around, the way was paved for double resentment: our missionary zeal has, moreover, led us so far from our traditional American pattern as to make people both at home and throughout the world wonder if we had not lost all sense of direction, if not, indeed, of decency.

We have long been known as a generous nation, a humane nation. Herbert Hoover's Belgian Relief mission had been for half a century the world's stereotype image of American compassion. It was reinforced by the outpourings of generosity through the American Red Cross whenever there was a disaster anywhere in the world; and the Marshall Plan aid after World War II, for all its political overtones, was an unprecedented act of magnanimity. Suddenly this humane nation conducts a war against the little countries of Indochina in a manner that shocks even our oldest friends among the nations of the world. More in hurt and disappointment than in anger, the people of these nations liken our tactics in Vietnam to the worst military atrocities in history.

The realization of the loss of sense of direction was a large part of what motivated our young in their disenchantment with the Establishment in all its forms. It has contributed to the general decline of confidence in all our institutions that is so clearly reflected in recent opinion surveys. What has come to be called a "crisis of confidence" is by no means limited to the young but is shared by all age groups.

Rather than wallowing in an orgy of self-immolation for our national sins, this is a time for a little mature, quiet soul-searching and redirecting of our cause. One of the glorious lessons of history—and it is no Pollyanna stuff, but the most solid of hard-rock fact—is that there is always another chance. The history books are filled with examples of nations and of individuals that have hit bottom in some form of defeat or even disgrace, then have picked themselves up off the ground and climbed back to positions of respect—all because they had the courage to work on building their way back.

One of the worst absurdities of the recent controversy over Vietnam was the fear so often expressed that we might "lose face" if we did less than win some kind of glorious victory. We suffered a much worse loss in losing a degree of respect and confidence in much of the world and among our own people—particularly the young. But we can regain all that and more if we will now conduct ourselves with poise and maturity.

The first step in that rebuilding is a renewal of our own faith in the values that brought us stature as a nation in the first place. Much of the idealism and inspiration has disappeared from even the vocabulary of our American policy, but, as Archibald MacLeish has suggested, they are by no means irretrievably lost.

> If you look closely and listen well, there is a human warmth, a human meaning which nothing has killed in almost twenty years and which nothing is likely to kill . . . What has always held this country together is an idea—a dream if you will—a large and abstract thought of the sort the realistic and the sophisticated may reject but mankind can hold to.

It is true that sophisticates may sneer at what is called "idealism," but we are at a point in history when there may be more earthy realism in idealist values than in either self-centered cynicism or self-satisfied missionary jingoism. Quoting again from Fulbright: "The foremost need of American foreign policy is a renewal of dedication to . . . a Lincolnian idea expressing that powerful strand of decency and humanity which is the true source of America's greatness."

Our obsession with being Number 1 is a sign of weakness and not of strength. Fifteen years ago we were a giant in a world of pigmies; today we are one among many strong, vital, healthy nations. To think that we could preserve our uniquely predominant position—even if it were desirable to do so—is a bit of ostrich-ism.

Again, though, it is not too late.

Step Number Two in the learning process is to realize that it is more mature, and hence stronger, to see ourselves in perspective: one of the Big Powers, perhaps the biggest, but still only one.

Above all, we are only one of all the nations, large and small.

Just as a democracy recognizes the dignity, the integrity, and the equality of every individual as a citizen, so do we need to recognize the dignity, integrity, and equality of rights of every nation. We have no charter from any source to be policeman of the world, or to be self-appointed guardian of the ideologies of the world.

We have no divine mission to "lead" the world, in the sense of imposing our beliefs, our values, our practices on other peoples.

When I testified before the Senate Foreign Relations Committee in opposition to our involvement in Vietnam, I raised the question, "Does the United States, from either a practical or a moral viewpoint, have either the right or the might to set itself up as the unilateral policeman of the world?" My own answer to that question was, and is, that such a position is morally indefensible and practically unsustainable.

If we want to change the structure or practices of the world, we should act as a good citizen would in his own community: we should work through the established machinery to seek the change. If there is no machinery for the particular change we want, we should work with our neighbors to create it.

Bigness imposes special obligations. They are the obligations of true leadership: to lead by example and by principle, not by force and coercion.

It is a lesson we learned in our own bank. We became the biggest in the world all within the lifetime of our founder, A. P. Giannini. While we were growing, and having to battle vigorously to compete with the long-established banks, we could get away with all manner of bumptious behavior. When we would do battle with the "giants of Wall Street," people would think it was amusing and would cheer us on. When A. P. would get front-page headlines for his blasts at Roosevelt and Morgenthau, people again would chuckle at the little bank man from our West talking so tough. But the minute we became the biggest, all that changed: what had been courageousness when we were small became arrogance when we were big. It was all right for little B. of A. to try to push the big boys around—that shook things up and was good for everybody—but if big B. of A. tried to do the same thing, it would have been throwing its weight around and acting like a bully.

Our country has been through a parallel experience of having to grow up to the responsibilities imposed by its newly gained strength and power.

Whether in a company or in a nation, when you become the biggest a new kind of leadership is expected of you. It is a leadership by example; a leadership in being humane; a leadership that is rational, that is flexible, and does not easily become ruffled. Above all, it is a leadership that stands up for what is morally and ethically right.

Human beings being what they are, this may seem an unrealistic task; but it is a moral imperative.

We learn in business that the thing we call "morale" is a sense of self-worth that grows out of the feeling of doing something worthwhile, of being identified with a company of which one can be proud, and of working under the direction of a leader whom one admires and who shows appreciation for one's work. Those are all ingredients of pride —pride in the best sense of that word. The same ingredients are needed for pride of country; and it was the damaging of some of those ingredients that caused the crisis of confidence that has concerned all thoughtful leaders.

There is nothing about this damaged morale, this crisis of confidence, that cannot be remedied; and the same remedy that will work at home will also operate to correct our damaged image abroad.

The remedy involves a change of attitude—the renewal of faith and rededication to principles that I mentioned earlier in this chapter—on the part of people at all levels in this country. Sounds impossibly starry-eyed, doesn't it? Don't believe for a moment that it is impossible. It is the very kind of thing that *can* be done, and I sense a vacuum, an unfilled yearning for something of the kind to be done.

It is not the sort of cause that has to wait for a Man on Horseback to come along and sound the call to arms. It would be infinitely helpful if there could be strong moral leadership at the head of our country to set the tone and point the way for the redirection of our national thinking; but in the present state of credibility gap I would expect this to be more of a welling-up from the bottom, led by not one but hundreds of local thought-leaders throughout the country. Everyone who reads this book, if he agrees with the premise, can play his part by generating discussion in all the circles in which he moves. Ultimately Congressional and other leaders of government are drawn into such discussion, and then ideas begin being translated into policies and policies into actions.

We got to where we are now largely by default and drift. I would prefer not to trust the drift to turn us around. I would rather see a lot of people pulling on oars. Fortunately, it is an exercise that can be expected to have good "side effects."

There is reason to believe that thoughtful people everywhere are prepared to accept the proposition that because the world has shrunk and because man has made giant leaps in his perceptions we now can agree that both as nations and as individuals we no longer need to base everything on outshining, dominating or out-acquiring one another; that we can focus on the good things that spell quality of life —which will take plenty of doing.

It may be said that all this runs counter to man's nature. But all civilized practices run counter to the uncivilized side of man.

THE SOIL OF LIBERTY

15

At stake in everything I have been discussing in these pages is something that is least mentioned in public discussion of current issues.

It is more important than the environment.

It is more important than profits, dividends, or wages.

It is usually taken for granted until it is lost—then it is too late.

It is our liberty.

When too much power is allowed to gravitate to central authority and then is allowed to be used autocratically, without recourse to democratic processes, the danger signals should flash. It is the classic pattern for surrender to tyranny.

In a book written by one who is at heart an optimist, and who has tried to convey in these pages his strong feeling of hope for this country in spite of the destructive forces that have been at work, it may seem strange to devote the final chapter to what must seem like an alarmist note. It is alarmist only in the sense that it is ringing a signal bell—an alert bell—but, depending on the response to the bell, it could foretell either danger or very good tidings.

I am not like Chicken Little of our childhood fable who

went running around yelling "The sky is falling! The sky is falling!" The sky is not falling; at least it is not going to fall tomorrow or the next day. But there is no use being naïve—particularly when doing the right thing can bring such positive rewards.

It is paradoxical that the very dangers we face bring into focus all the highest principles that are inherent in a good society; that we could reach such a watershed peak that there are only two choices: in one direction we would face a condition that has never been dreamed of in this Sweet Land of Liberty—the loss of that Liberty; and yet in the other direction we can find a better life than most of us have known. Yet it is true.

There is no use shutting our eyes to the dangers. Only if we recognize and identify them can we focus on what we need to do to avoid them. And there is plenty that can be done; this is not a gloomy prediction of inescapable doom.

Democracy is not easy to maintain. It has prevailed in only brief periods of history; in fact, the Durants say, "Democracies have been hectic interludes." But they have been precious interludes, and they no longer have to be only interludes if we are willing to use our tremendous resources of knowledge and understanding to preserve and prolong the one we have inherited.

Except for sudden invasion by a foreign power, when liberty has been lost anywhere, at any time, it was always possible to look back and see that the signals had been clear for a long time.

I have so much faith in the native good sense of the American people and in their basic dedication to freedom— even though that dedication has been pretty dormant for quite a spell now—that I think they would wake up to the fatal trend before it was too late. It is only in a spirit of extra caution that I suggest that if we all can recognize the symptoms we shall be even more certain to avoid the dread disease.

For those who say, "It can't happen here," let me first point out what some of the danger signals are. Reading history we see that the classic symptoms of the viruses that can attack liberty are visible all around us today. At first glance they might seem unrelated, but there is a thread of common principle running through all of this.

Attacks on freedom of the press have come from some of the very quarters where that freedom should be most stoutly defended as one of our basic freedoms under the Bill of Rights. Irresponsible behavior by the press is irritating and at times infuriating even to those who are not its victims, but it is not new in this country and can do little harm as long as there can be freedom of expression by an opposition press.

Bullying and browbeating the press and jailing newspapermen for not revealing their sources will inevitably jeopardize the free flow of information that the First Amendment was intended to promote.

The "bugging" at Watergate and elsewhere might be laughed off as infantile if its sponsorship did not have such sinister overtones. Spying and espionage by the party in power smacks so much of Gestapo methods and are so foreign to the American tradition as to be frightening—as well as nauseating in their stupidity under the circumstances in which they were used.

The isolation of national leaders from exposure to the press would be bad enough if viewed only in terms of the immediate effects: shutting off a vital source of news, interpretation, and comment. But what it implies is infinitely worse: that these people consider themselves above the need for public accountability.

The callousness toward human life displayed by our national leaders in the use of antipersonnel weapons against civilians in Vietnam may seem remote from domestic liberties in the United States, but it is the mark of potential despotism. It is, moreover, only an extension of the state of mind that would be comfortable in such cavalier disregard of Congress in the entire conduct of that war. The "angry temper" bombing of 1972 was an exaggerated expression of that same mental state.

In general, this group of symptoms involves the arrogance of power—the same virus, in a different form, that has infected our foreign relations.

Lest our youth who were so critical—and properly so—of the war in Indochina feel too self-righteous, let me remind them that in their violent protests against the immorality of the war many of them were guilty of endangering the very values they were proclaiming.

Both young and old must recognize that liberty is indivisible.

We might have had another eruption from a related virus, but restraint avoided it.

We averted the threat of vigilantism or of real police-state suppression during the campus uprisings of 1969–70 as we had earlier in the ghetto riots of 1964. But the pressures and clamor for both kinds of action were a warning that just as the riots got out of hand so could the counter measures. I am aware of the charges, many of them true, of police excesses during those riots; but those were excesses and aberrations from an orderly, lawful system—quite a different animal from a real Gestapo-style takeover.

Our forces of law, justice, and protection have an equally heavy burden of responsibility on their shoulders today in dealing with the wave of crime that is terrorizing large sections of America. It is germane to this discussion of liberty because nowhere in history has there been liberty without order under law. History also records the typical pattern of rampant crime, the breakdown and impotence of efforts at law enforcement, followed by the "strong man" who seizes the reigns of power to put down the lawlessness.

I am distressed by the downgrading of the term "law and order." Minority groups have equated the term with repressive police-state tactics and have persuaded most urban-affairs bodies like the Urban Coalition to drop the use of the phrase in favor of something like "law and justice." Further support for this denigration comes from people like Rollo May, psychoanalyst and author, who says that too much emphasis on law and order leads to violence.

It is true that at times when regularly constituted law enforcement has been lacking or has broken down and people have "taken the law into their own hands," as so often happened in the pioneer days of the West, it was done in the name of law and order. It is also true that there have been countless abuses and excesses committed in the name of law and order, and that the enforcement of the law should be done with justice and fairness. But it also is true that unless it *is* enforced, the law alone provides no justice.

As I write these words, my morning paper has just reported the results of a national survey showing that one person in three in America's urban areas was robbed, mugged, or suffered property loss in 1972. Without professing expertise in how to prevent crime, I would simply say that if we value liberty, we had better give high priority, in our social concerns, to the right to walk the streets in safety.

There is another cluster of symptoms. (The doctors might call it a "syndrome.") They involve large parts of our populace looking to government for security or for subsidy.

Each of the forms of subsidy to an industry had a good rational basis at the time it was first enacted. Many of them intended to meet an emergency situation and were presumably temporary. When the farm subsidies, for example, were first put into effect during the Great Depression, the markets for many of our major crops had collapsed; competition from other countries was pushing us out of some world markets; and bankruptcy seemed to threaten the very foundations of what was still a predominantly agricultural nation.

Forty years, though, can hardly be called a period of emergency, and to have continued those subsidies through the greatest boom and prosperity in history is the height of absurdity.

The sheer cost in higher taxes of these and the many other types of subsidy has been bad enough, but it has not been the worst of the bad effects. Much worse has been the fact that each time any attempt is made to correct one of the other programs that is eating away the foundations of a healthy society the lobby for that program can throw up a smoke screen about "billion-dollar handouts to the giant farming corporations, oil companies, and airlines while children are left in poverty."

Another effect worse than the immediate dollar cost is the spreading habit of looking to the government—to the federal government mainly—for solution of all problems.

That is what is most nightmarish about the Welfare Nightmare. No one in a humane country proposes to see anyone starve, but that is not the issue here. When the same family has continued on welfare for three generations —again spanning the greatest periods of prosperity in history—it is not merely because *those people* wanted to stay on welfare but because among other things we have built up a colossal machinery to encourage them to stay on.

When I say that the network of social workers and administrators has created a welfare class because it is more to the advantage of this bureaucracy to foster dependency among the recipients than to help make them independent —and that is true—I am not laying all the blame on the shoulders of the welfare bureaucracy. The rest of us must share that blame because we have gone on electing people to Congress and to the White House who were willing to trade on human weakness—to seek votes by playing on that human appetite for "something for nothing."

In this as in many of the other problems plaguing us—
our inflation at home, our balance of payments and dollar-
devaluation problems abroad—we all are paying the price
for a woeful lack of discipline. We cannot point a finger of
shame at someone else and say "he did it," because we all
collectively have been playing this game of "something for
nothing." We have been willing to countenance spending
programs domestically and all over the globe, and we haven't
been willing to tax ourselves to pay for them. We have been
like an individual (we all have known him) who goes on a
spending spree without money enough to pay for what he
has bought. His credit suffers; our dollar suffered.

Our unbalanced budgets, year after year in the face of
unprecedented prosperity, have been a sign of miserable
irresponsibility. Not someone else's irresponsibility—ours.
We tolerated it.

All this may seem remote from the issue of liberty until
we bring it home to something else we all have tolerated
with scarcely a whimper: the imposition of economic controls, wage and price controls.

If anyone had predicted a generation ago that the American people, in peacetime, would consent to controls over so
much of their economic lives, few would have believed him.
Yet when it came, people not only accepted but welcomed
it. So far had we come down the road of dependency on
government that we were willing to surrender another large
measure of freedom for a degree of material protection and
security.

We had forgotten the lesson recited in 1759 by Benjamin
Franklin: "Those who would give up essential liberty to
purchase a little temporary safety deserve neither liberty
nor safety."

It may be argued, I know, that we were not "in peacetime" when the controls were imposed; that ours was in
fact, if not in name, a war economy; and that the effects of
the war had brought us to a state of economic emergency

that gave us no choice but to take some such action. That reasoning only highlights what was one of the root causes of our economic crisis: that we had gone all through the period of the Vietnam build-up and massive military engagement without our political leaders showing the courage, or our citizens showing the discipline, to face up to the cold, hard fact of life that if we were going to spend the money on that engagement and not feed the fires of inflation, we had to pay for it either by more taxes or less spending on other purposes. Spending without taxing is the classic road to inflation, and we had taken it. The fact that we had begun to wind down our involvement in Vietnam before the economic emergency reached crisis proportions and the controls were imposed adds very little to the argument.

In any case, it is not my purpose in this book to go into a lengthy discussion of whether any alternatives remained open at that late hour—whether the politically distasteful measures of fiscal and monetary policy that were not used might have served the country better than the politically expedient steps that were taken. What *is* germane to the thesis of this chapter is that those alternatives were not even discussed; that the controls were announced, everyone acquiesced in them—and that was that.

The further fact that two years later, as this book is being written, the controls still are not working successfully—as such controls never have worked except in a *totally* controlled economy—is simply another disturbing reminder that piecemeal surrenders of liberty to gain temporary shelter from danger do not avoid the inevitable day of reckoning.

Apathy and self-interest are twin threats to the preservation of freedoms.

So much for the danger signals, the symptoms of the disease we want to avoid. How do we avoid it?

It can be done—if we are willing to make the right choices. I almost said, "If we are willing to pay the price," but for every difficult choice that apparently has a high price tag the rewards are so high that there is no net cost.

The first choice is just a decision: to recognize that if we want liberty, we must really *want* it—want it enough to exact from ourselves the discipline that will be needed.

We shall need discipline in all the things we must do collectively. That includes all the fiscal and other economic decisions we must make to put our nation back into a solvent and self-respecting condition.

We shall need discipline and restraint individually, so that when we are offered options by political candidates or others we will turn our backs on any expedient course that would chip away the foundations of our free society.

We shall need, in all our individual and collective choices, a renewed emphasis on something we don't hear talked about very much lately; something called character. We need to demand it of those who represent us in government and of all those who hold positions of trust anywhere: government, business, the professions. We need to demand it of ourselves. When our young speak of their loss of confidence in our institutions and in our leadership, this is what they are talking about. They don't often use the word character, but they speak of honesty, which is the first essential of character.

People say, "You can't turn back the clock," but in seeking guidance on matters of character and conduct the only place we can safely look is backward over the ages to see what has stood the test of time. Paradoxically, some of the "new values" growing up in this country are in fact a turning back of the clock, a return to time-tested principles that are older than our present society.

Toffler scoffs at Herbert Spencer's maintaining that "Education has for its object the formation of character." This, says Toffler, means the seduction or terrorization of the young into the value systems of the old. Here Toffler misses, I believe, one of the lessons of history. Education *can* be what Toffler describes, but the best education is not. In actual fact, the recent generations of youth have been seduced and terrorized, not only in school but at home and everywhere, by television, radio, newspaper, and billboard, by every form of communication, to lure them into the value systems of the *current generation* of the old. But that is quite different from exposing them to the best thinking of the ages, which may indeed often be contradictory but which can be seen in the context of its time and can then offer the young a basis for choice. That is an essential of education and that, I am sure, is more nearly what Spencer had in mind.

The young have decried the hypocrisy that called for Puritan morality in some matters of purely personal conduct—where, in their eyes, a departure from that code harmed no one but the doer—but seemed to condone sharp and questionable practices that robbed and cheated thousands of others.

We could well take a cue from them in the standards of conduct that we endeavor to set for our society. If we want our society to survive, and yet to have the freedom and the vibrance that will make it worth preserving, we shall need to make a sharp separation between two sets of values. In all those areas in which one person's conduct affects the well-being of another—whether it be conduct by the President of the United States, the executive of a corporation, a policeman on his beat, or one citizen neighboring another—we should expect the kind of regard for other human beings that calls for honesty of dealing, honesty of expression, and respect for the person and the rights of others. Only with such regards for others do we have the foundation for a free society; and with the necessary respect for fellow humans, we have the right to demand strict, uncompromising conformity.

To hark back again to my "base-line" concept, I am convinced that human progress results from repeatedly raising the level of consensus as to what is acceptable conduct. Our generation can jack up that level another notch by letting our leaders—those who hold high positions anywhere in our society—know that we will accept nothing less than this standard of integrity.

In all other areas, where each person's conduct affects only himself, we should not only tolerate but encourage the greatest of individuality. I find something entirely compatible between young people's insistence on freedom to do their own thing and my belief in the mosaic theory, as distinguished from the melting-pot theory.

Early in this century, when immigration was a greater relative factor than it is today, we heard a great deal about America being a melting pot. A book by Israel Zangwill entitled *The Melting Pot* focused national attention on the phenomenon, unique in history on any such scale, of immigrants coming to America from all parts of the world, bringing with them their separate customs, language, traditions, religion, culture, and other backgrounds. These were then melted together to form one new American character and culture.

Granting the tremendous strengths that each of these blood- and culture-streams has added to American life; and granting that each of these new Americans had an obligation to assume his role as an American and not remain forever an alien visitor here, I never had thought that it was necessary for these people all to be "melted down" into one single common-denominator alloy. I have resisted the thought that all the richness of their ancestral history must be incinerated away. I have preferred to think of them as a great mosaic in which their differences of cultural heritage add color and beauty and variety to our American scene.

In actual fact, this has happened in all communities fortunate enough to have a clustering of people with recent foreign backgrounds. As one whose own parents were Swedish immigrants, I can testify that no Colonial Dame or Daughter of the American Revolution could ever have been prouder of American citizenship—or more willing to work at it—than these people who had *chosen* to be Americans. And their serving of Swedish foods or decorating their houses with bits of Swedish craftsmanship no more diluted their Americanism than did one neighbor's liking to play the piccolo while another preferred to go duck-hunting.

Life in this country was in many respects more interesting when our immigration was still a newer thing and the sharper differences between people of different origins were still more evident. This mosaic pattern was always more distinct and continued longer in our metropolitan areas than it did in some of our inland small towns, where the stigma of being "foreign" brought more pressure to conform.

I think it is important that people of different national origins, like people who differ in any other respect, have equal opportunity to develop their own potentials economically, culturally, socially, and every other way. If we enhance, rather than suppress, opportunities for people to develop their different individualities interestingly and satisfyingly to themselves, the result will be enriching to all of us.

There is a price we all should pay for this privilege of being ourselves and doing our own thing. From my childhood years on a homestead farm, I learned the lesson that we must put back into the soil as much as we take out. Instead of our looking only to someone else to solve society's problems; instead of clamoring only for *corporate* social responsibility, or for *government* action on every crisis, we should ask ourselves:

What have I done to help, even a little bit, on any of the problems I am fussing about?

How much have I put back into the soil of America that has yielded so much to me?

How good has my stewardship been?

When I am through, will I leave my part of this world in as good condition as when I entered it?

INDEX

151